McGraw-Hill Education

Vocabulary

Grades 3–5

Second Edition

McGraw-Hill Education

Vocabulary

Grades 3–5
Second Edition

Gary Robert Muschla

New York   Chicago   San Francisco   Athens   London   Madrid
Mexico City   Milan   New Delhi   Singapore   Sydney   Toronto

First edition published under the name *Practice Makes Perfect: Exploring Vocabulary,
Ages 8–12*.

8 9   LHS   23 22 21 20

ISBN   978-1-260-13519-0
MHID   1-260-13519-5

e-ISBN   978-1-260-13520-6
e-MHID   1-260-13520-9

Interior design by Nick Panos

McGraw-Hill Education books are available at special quantity discounts to use as
premiums and sales promotions or for use in corporate training programs. To contact a
representative, please visit the Contact Us page at www.mhprofessional.com.

Contents

About This Book

Words are the foundation of reading, speaking, and writing. It is through words that we share ideas and learn new things. The understanding and use of words—your vocabulary—relate directly to learning. Students who have rich vocabularies usually do better in school than students whose vocabularies are poor.

The lessons in this book provide more than 500 words that are found in third-, fourth-, and fifth-grade curriculums. The definitions of these words include more words that can expand vocabulary even further. Many of the words throughout this book appear on standardized tests.

McGraw-Hill Education's *Vocabulary Grades 3-5* can be a helpful resource for learning the meanings and uses of words. This new edition of the book retains all of the lessons and valued features of the first edition, while extending its scope with new lessons and vocabulary words. Like the original edition (published under the title *Practice Makes Perfect: Exploring Vocabulary, Ages 8-12*), this book can be used by both students and teachers. Students (working alone or with their parents) can complete the lessons, while teachers will find the materials of the book useful for classroom instruction.

Having a broad vocabulary is a key to being successful in school and beyond. It is my hope that this book will make the study of vocabulary an enjoyable experience.

How to Use This Book

Vocabulary Grades 3-5 contains 45 lessons. Each lesson focuses on a particular type of word or word group. Each includes a list of words and three practice worksheets. An alphabetical list of the words in the lessons and an answer key for the worksheets conclude the book.

Each lesson begins with a list of words students should know. Most lessons present 10 words, but a few present more. For most lessons, words are shown with their part of speech, definition, and a sample sentence. A Vocabulary Tip is also included. Students should study the list of words and their definitions for each lesson before trying to do the worksheets. If any words in the definitions are unfamiliar, they should use a dictionary to check the meanings of those words. Learning these words, along with the words presented in the lesson, will expand vocabulary greatly.

The worksheets are designed to make learning vocabulary easy and fun. Each worksheet begins with a question that students can answer by completing the worksheet correctly. They should try to complete the worksheets without looking back at the definitions of the list words, and look back only if they need help.

Completing the worksheets in this book will help students to build their vocabulary. But there are many other ways they can learn new words and their meanings:

- Read. Reading builds vocabulary. Read different kinds of selections: novels, short stories, nonfiction books, and magazines. Make reading a habit.
- Use context clues to find the meanings of new words. You can often figure out the meaning of a word by the way it is used in a sentence. Look for clues in the following:
  - Examples that give the meaning of a new word
  - Familiar words and phrases that hint at the meaning of a new word
  - Phrases after new words that contain their definitions
  - Synonyms and antonyms that help you understand the meaning of new words
- When necessary, use a dictionary to find the meanings of new words.
- When you learn a new word, note if it has multiple meanings. Many words do. Try to learn the different meanings of new words.
- Learn the meanings of prefixes and suffixes. Prefixes and suffixes alter the meanings of words. Use your understanding of prefixes and suffixes to help you understand the meanings of the words to which they are attached.
- When you learn a new word, repeat it and its meaning silently to yourself. Think of how the word is related to other words. This will help you to remember it.
- Think of a new word's synonyms and antonyms. This will broaden your understanding of the word.
- Write down new words and their meanings in a "New Words" notebook. Review your notebook from time to time to refresh your memory.
- Use a thesaurus to find the synonyms of words.
- Do word games such as crossword puzzles.
- Look for new words wherever you go, every day, and in every subject in school.

Encourage students to make new words a part of their vocabulary and use them in speaking, reading, and writing.

Synonyms, I

A synonym is a word that has the same or about the same meaning as another word.

1. gigantic (adj): big; huge; massive

   Many dinosaurs were <u>gigantic</u> creatures.

2. liberty (n): freedom; independence

   The colonists fought for <u>liberty</u> during the Revolutionary War.

3. outstanding (adj): noteworthy; famous; important

   Jason made an <u>outstanding</u> catch in the baseball game.

4. awkward (adj): clumsy; ungraceful

   Maria felt <u>awkward</u> learning the new dance.

5. common (adj): usual; frequent

   Freezing temperatures are <u>common</u> in winter.

6. cute (adj): pretty; attractive

   Everyone loved the <u>cute</u> little kitten.

7. entire (adj): whole; complete

   We spent our <u>entire</u> vacation in Florida.

8. divide (v): separate; split

   We will <u>divide</u> the bill for lunch equally.

9. startle (v): alarm; frighten

   Lightning and thunder will <u>startle</u> the puppy.

10. comical (adj): funny; amusing

    The clown's act was <u>comical</u>.

Vocabulary Tip

A thesaurus is an excellent resource for finding synonyms.

1.1 Fearsome Sea Creature

This sea creature is one of the world's most fearsome predators. What is it?

   To answer the question, match each word on the left with its synonym on the right. Write the letter of each answer in the space above the word's number at the bottom of the page. You will need to divide the letters into words.

Words

1. common _____

2. entire _____

3. comical _____

4. gigantic _____

5. liberty _____

6. awkward _____

7. startle _____

8. cute _____

9. outstanding _____

10. divide _____

Synonyms

G. noteworthy

H. separate

S. freedom

T. usual

I. frighten

E. complete

K. attractive

W. amusing

R. clumsy

A. huge

___ ___ ___ ___ ___ ___ ___ ___ ___ ___ ___ ___ ___ ___
 9   6   2   4   1   3   10 7   1   2   5   10 4   6   8

1.2 First and Last

This American colony was the first to declare its independence from Great Britain in 1776. It was also the last of the original 13 colonies to ratify the Constitution in 1790. What was the name of this colony?

To answer the question, complete each sentence with the correct word. Choose your answers from the words after the sentences. Write the letter of each answer in the space above its sentence number at the bottom of the page. You will need to divide the letters into words. One letter is provided.

1. Americans fought the Revolutionary War to gain their _____.

2. The baby hugged the _____ little teddy bear.

3. Susan was named student writer of the month for her _____ story.

4. We laughed throughout the _____ TV show.

5. Hot summers are _____ in Arizona.

6. Because of heavy traffic, we spent the _____ day driving to grandmother's house.

7. The little boy planned to _____ his mother with the frog.

8. The puppy's first steps were _____ , and he quickly stumbled.

9. The teacher instructed her students to _____ into groups.

10. Compared with mice, elephants are _____ animals.

Answers

L. gigantic
A. liberty
N. common
H. awkward
S. outstanding

O. cute
I. entire
R. divide
D. startle
E. comical

__ __ __ D __ __ __ __ __ __ __
9   8   2   4   6   3 10   1   5   7

1.3 A Deadly Sting

This creature lives in the waters north of Australia. Its tentacles can grow to be 15 feet (about 5 meters) long, and its sting can be deadly. What is it?

To answer the question, read each sentence below. Replace each underlined word with its synonym. Choose your answers from the words after each sentence. Write the letter of each answer in the space above its sentence number at the bottom of the page. Some letters are provided.

1. The Pacific Ocean, the largest ocean on earth, is <u>gigantic</u>.
   S. deep   O. huge   T. noteworthy

2. We will <u>divide</u> the cards into groups.
   U. complete   I. count   E. separate

3. Thunderstorms are <u>common</u> during this time of year.
   P. famous   S. powerful   Y. usual

4. Judy Blume is one of the most <u>outstanding</u> writers of children's books.
   A. frequent   I. famous   E. complete

5. We ate the <u>entire</u> pizza ourselves.
   F. whole   P. big   W. tasty

6. Tripping on your untied shoelaces is an <u>awkward</u> moment.
   G. massive   X. ungraceful   T. amusing

7. The rebels fought for <u>liberty</u> during the war.
   E. wealth   D. power   J. freedom

8. The baby was <u>cute</u> in her Halloween costume.
   L. pretty   T. silly   P. smiling

9. The sudden sound of a smoke alarm will <u>startle</u> anyone.
   T. wake   D. call   H. alarm

10. The silly puppy's playful actions were <u>comical</u>.
    T. interesting   B. amusing   R. ungraceful

__	__	__		__	__	L	__	__	__	__	S	__
10	1	6		7	2		8	3	5	4		9

Synonyms, II

A synonym is a word that has the same or about the same meaning as another word.

1. immense (adj): vast; tremendous; gigantic

   Mount Everest, the highest mountain in the world, is <u>immense</u>.

2. powerful (adj): strong; mighty

   The <u>powerful</u> storm caused great destruction.

3. rage (n): anger; fury; wrath

   The <u>rage</u> of the storm was frightening.

4. remain (v): stay; wait; to continue in the same state

   Tara must <u>remain</u> in bed as long as she has a fever.

5. conflict (n): struggle; battle; fight; war

   The <u>conflict</u> between the two countries lasted for years.

6. marvelous (adj): wonderful; astonishing; extraordinary

   Jason enjoyed a <u>marvelous</u> show at the planetarium.

7. tiny (adj): small; little

   A flea is so <u>tiny</u> that it is difficult to see.

8. revise (v): rewrite; change; alter

   Professional authors always <u>revise</u> their work.

9. ferocious (adj): savage; fierce; cruel

   The <u>ferocious</u> dragon attacked the village.

10. boundary (n): border; edge; margin

   The Rio Grande is a river that serves as the <u>boundary</u> between the United States and Mexico.

Vocabulary Tip

Learning the synonyms of words is an excellent way to improve your vocabulary.

Synonyms, II

2.1 Smart Dogs

Many dog breeders agree that these two dogs are the smartest of all breeds. One is the Jack Russell terrier. What is the other?

To answer the question, find the synonym of each word below. Choose your answers from the choices that follow each word. Write the letter of each answer in the space above its line number at the bottom of the page. One letter is provided.

1. tiny:	R. little	S. average	Y. large
2. powerful:	E. wonderful	O. strong	I. nice
3. ferocious:	S. slow	I. savage	E. light
4. remain:	I. leave	E. stay	A. hurry
5. marvelous:	D. frightful	G. dangerous	S. wonderful
6. rage:	O. tough	H. thoughtful	C. anger
7. revise:	T. change	L. begin	P. finish
8. immense:	S. calm	R. divide	B. vast
9. boundary:	H. border	D. outside	N. line
10. conflict:	P. think	L. fight	T. discover

```
__ __ __ __ __ __ __ __   __ __ __   D __ __   __ __ __ __ __ __
5  6  2  7  7  3  5  9    8  2  1    4  1    6  2  10 10 3  4
```

8

2.2 The Name's the Same

Portland is the largest city in two states of the United States. What are these states?

To answer the question, read each sentence below. Replace each underlined word with its synonym. Choose your answers from the words after the each sentence. Write the letter of each answer in the space above its sentence number at the bottom of the page. You will need to divide the letters into words. Some letters are provided.

1. The king's <u>rage</u> at the bad news was terrifying to his people.
   A. roar   E. anger   O. frown

2. I had to <u>revise</u> my story three times before I was happy with it.
   N. research   U. illustrate   R. rewrite

3. A fence marks the <u>boundary</u> between our yard and our neighbor's yard.
   A. border   U. garden   O. conflict

4. Mark decided to <u>remain</u> in the library until his mother came to pick him up.
   I. read   A. stay   E. study

5. The rocket's <u>powerful</u> engines lifted it into space.
   O. mighty   U. noisy   R. fantastic

6. A tsunami can grow to be an <u>immense</u> wave and cause great destruction.
   S. alarming   E. ocean   I. gigantic

7. We had a <u>marvelous</u> time at the party.
   N. wonderful   D. interesting   S. boring

8. It was hard to believe that the <u>tiny</u> puppy would one day grow to be a Saint Bernard.
   J. cute   M. small   R. cuddly

9. With a <u>ferocious</u> snarl, the monster came toward us.
   P. mysterious   G. fierce   S. gigantic

10. The argument quickly led to a <u>conflict</u>.
    N. margin   D. fight   K. rage

__ __ __ N __ __ N __ O __ E __ __ __
8   4   6   1   3   10   2   9   5   7

Synonyms, II

© Gary Robert Muschla

9

2.3 First Named Dinosaur

Megalosaurus was a large, meat-eating dinosaur. It was the first dinosaur to be given a scientific name. An Englishman named it in 1824. Who was he?

To answer the question, complete each sentence with the correct word. Choose your answers from the words after the sentences. Write the letter of each answer in the space above its sentence number at the bottom of the page. One letter is provided.

1. We decided to _____ at Walt Disney World for two more days.

2. Rashid must _____ his report.

3. The town stood in the shadow of the _____ mountain.

4. The _____ between Canada and the lower 48 states of the United States is 3,987 miles (6,416 kilometers) long.

5. Conner was able to see Jupiter through the _____ telescope.

6. Mice can squeeze through _____ holes.

7. Every good story has _____ between the hero and the villain.

8. The little boy's sudden _____ was calmed as soon as he got his own way.

9. The lion's _____ growl caused the herd of zebras to run.

10. The graceful dancers put on a _____ show.

Answers

K. immense
N. powerful
D. rage
A. remain
L. conflict
B. marvelous
C. revise
W. ferocious
I. tiny
M. boundary

__ __ __ __ __ __ __   __ U __ __ __ __ __ __
9 6 7 7 6 1 4   10   2 3 7 1 5 8

Synonyms, II

Antonyms, I

An antonym is a word that has the opposite, or nearly opposite, meaning of another word.

1. failure (n): defeat; not being successful

   Antonyms: success; triumph; achievement

   The team's <u>failure</u> to follow their game plan led to the loss of the championship.

2. firm (adj): hard; solid; steady

   Antonyms: soft; unstable

   The foundation for the stage was <u>firm</u>.

3. dangerous (adj): unsafe; harmful

   Antonyms: safe; harmless

   The old wooden bridge looked <u>dangerous</u>.

4. cheap (adj): inexpensive; costing little; of poor quality

   Antonyms: expensive; costly

   Because of the big sale, all of the DVDs were <u>cheap</u>.

5. obey (v): to follow orders; to heed

   Antonyms: disobey; defy; ignore

   It is important to <u>obey</u> safety rules.

6. argue (v): to disagree; to quarrel; to dispute

   Antonyms: agree; accept; consent

   Lisa and her sister sometimes <u>argue</u> over silly things.

7. doubt (v): to be unsure; to question; to disbelieve

   Antonyms: believe; trust

   With the warm temperatures, I <u>doubt</u> it will snow.

8. special (adj): unusual; rare; uncommon   Antonyms: common; usual

    In our family, birthdays are <u>special</u> days.

9. avoid (v): to stay away from; to keep out of the way of; to dodge   Antonyms: meet; welcome; face

    Using sunscreen is a way to <u>avoid</u> sunburn.

10. spacious (adj): roomy; ample; sizable   Antonyms: cramped; crowded; small

    Our hotel room was <u>spacious</u> and comfortable.

Vocabulary Tip

Along with synonyms, a thesaurus often contains antonyms of words.

Antonyms, I

3.1 Left-Handed Animal

Just like people, animals may be right-handed or left-handed (or right-pawed or left-pawed). Many wildlife experts believe that all members of a certain species are left-handed. What are these animals?

To answer the question, find the meaning of each word below. Choose your answers from the choices that follow each word. Write the letter of each answer in the space above its line number at the bottom of the page. You will need to divide the letters into words.

1. special: A. kind   E. unusual   U. element

2. firm: R. solid   T. heavy   D. support

3. obey: E. compare   A. heed   O. break

4. failure: Y. believe   I. example   A. defeat

5. avoid: D. strike   N. gather   S. dodge

6. dangerous: O. harmful   I. result   H. enjoyable

7. spacious: E. thoughtful   R. roomy   T. small

8. doubt: H. honesty   S. humor   B. disbelieve

9. cheap: L. inexpensive   E. sale   O. tough

10. argue: S. awful   P. disagree   T. agree

__ __ __ __ __ __ __ __ __ __
10   6   9   4   2   8   1   3   7   5

Antonyms, I

13

3.2 A Tiny Animal

This little mammal weighs about the same as a dime. It is generally thought to be the smallest mammal in North America. What is it?

To answer the question, match each word on the left with its antonym on the right. Write the letter of each answer in the space above the word's number at the bottom of the page.

Words	Antonyms
1. cheap _____	Y. harmless
2. special _____	T. defy
3. failure _____	P. cramped
4. avoid _____	M. meet
5. argue _____	H. soft
6. obey _____	S. success
7. firm _____	E. trust
8. spacious _____	G. usual
9. dangerous _____	R. costly
10. doubt _____	W. agree

__ __ __   __ __ __ __ __   __ __ __ __ __
6 7 10   8 9 2 4 9   3 7 1 10 5

3.3 Little Birds

Hummingbirds are the smallest of all birds. They are so small that one of their enemies is an insect. What is the name of this insect?

To answer the question, correct the sentences by replacing each underlined word with its antonym. Choose your answers from the words after the sentences. Write the letter of each answer in the space above its sentence number at the bottom of the page.

1. The <u>cheap</u> ring sparkled in the light.

2. It is <u>safe</u> to drive on icy roads.

3. After the heavy rain, the ground was <u>firm</u>.

4. Puppies must learn to <u>ignore</u> the commands of their owners.

5. The launch of the new spacecraft was a <u>failure</u>.

6. The students were surprised by the <u>usual</u> announcement in the middle of the day.

7. The rooms of their new home were <u>small</u>.

8. Tonya was excited to <u>avoid</u> her new baby sister.

9. Tom and his brother get along well and usually <u>argue</u> a lot.

10. Having plenty of evidence that he stole the bicycle, the police officers <u>believe</u> the thief's claim of innocence.

Answers

Y. obey   M. doubt
N. soft   G. meet
T. expensive   R. dangerous
S. special   I. spacious
P. agree   A. success

__	__	__	__	__	__	__		__	__	__	__	__	__
9	2	5	4	7	3	8		10	5	3	1	7	6

Antonyms, I

15

Antonyms, II

An antonym is a word that has the opposite, or nearly opposite, meaning of another word.

1. humorous (adj): funny; amusing;   Antonyms: serious; grave; stern
   comical

   We laughed through much of the <u>humorous</u> movie.

2. brave (adj): courageous; fearless   Antonyms: cowardly; fearful; timid

   The <u>brave</u> knight saved the princess.

3. interesting (adj): being able to   Antonyms: boring; dull;
   hold one's attention; engaging   uninteresting

   I could not stop reading because the book was so <u>interesting</u>.

4. delightful (adj): enjoyable; pleasant;   Antonyms: unpleasant; distasteful
   pleasing

   We had a <u>delightful</u> trip to the city and cannot wait to return.

5. destroy (v): to ruin; to wreck;   Antonyms: create; make; build
   to tear down

   The incoming tide will <u>destroy</u> the sand castle.

6. gather (v): to bring together;   Antonyms: separate; scatter
   to collect

   We had to <u>gather</u> materials for our project.

7. polite (adj): courteous; having good manners

   Antonyms: rude; discourteous; fresh

   Everyone at the meeting was friendly and <u>polite</u>.

8. agree (v): to consent; to accept

   Antonyms: reject; deny; refuse; disagree

   Jonathan and Thomas <u>agree</u> on a name for their puppy.

9. loyalty (n): devotion; faithfulness

   Antonyms: disloyalty; treachery

   The soldiers showed great <u>loyalty</u> to their commander.

10. nonsense (n): foolishness; silliness; something that does not make sense

    Antonyms: sense; fact; logic

    Uncle Bill believes that stories of beings from other planets are <u>nonsense</u>.

Vocabulary Tip

Understanding the antonyms of words expands your vocabulary.

4.1 An Original Name

The Portuguese explorer Ferdinand Magellan named the Pacific Ocean in 1520. What was the original meaning of the Pacific Ocean's name?

To answer the question, complete each sentence with the correct word. Choose your answers from the words after each sentence. Write the letter of each answer in the space above its sentence number at the end of the exercise. You will need to divide the letters into words. One letter is provided.

1. The program about volcanoes was _____ and held everyone's attention.
   E. nonsense   I. polite   U. interesting

2. The new student was very _____ and showed good manners all day.
   E. polite   S. brave   M. rude

3. The _____ firefighters saved the woman from the burning building.
   T. humorous   C. brave   R. delightful

4. The tornado will _____ anything in its path.
   A. destroy   E. agree   S. gather

5. The audience applauded the students' _____ performance at the winter concert.
   D. disappointing   T. nonsense   F. delightful

6. Grandfather always told _____ stories that made us laugh.
   N. chilling   S. humorous   P. brave

7. Mrs. Taylor told her students to _____ their belongings before leaving for home.
   E. gather   U. separate   I. accept

8. Mr. Green does not believe in dragons and says stories about them are _____.
   T. serious   P. nonsense   S. real

9. The students of each group must _____ on a topic for their project.
   H. collect   L. agree   M. wreck

10. George Washington's _____ to the new country was clear to everyone.

A. loyalty   Y. nonsense   O. brave

$$\underline{\hspace{1em}} \quad \underline{\hspace{1em}} \quad \underline{\hspace{1em}} \quad \underline{\hspace{1em}} \quad \underline{\text{E}} \quad \underline{\hspace{1em}} \quad \underline{\hspace{1em}} \quad \underline{\hspace{1em}} \quad \underline{\hspace{1em}} \quad \underline{\hspace{1em}} \quad \underline{\hspace{1em}}$$
$$8 \quad\; 2 \quad 10 \quad\; 3 \qquad\quad\; 5 \quad\; 1 \quad\; 9 \quad\; 6 \quad\; 7 \quad\; 4$$

4.2 Fleas

Fleas are small, wingless insects. They live on the skin of animals, especially mammals. Fleas feed on the blood of their hosts. What are people who are experts on fleas called?

To answer the question, find the antonym of each word below. Choose your answers from the choices that follow each word. Write the letter of the antonym in the space above its line number at the bottom of the page. Some letters are provided.

1. destroy: C. build   S. wreck   K. collect

2. polite: D. agree   M. foolishness   G. rude

3. nonsense: U. silliness   E. dull   I. sense

4. humorous: I. serious   E. fearless   A. amusing

5. delightful: P. interesting   L. unpleasant   N. comical

6. brave: R. boring   P. cowardly   T. courageous

7. agree: O. reject   A. polite   Y. create

8. loyalty: S. faithfulness   T. treachery   D. logic

9. gather: L. scatter   S. delight   N. collect

10. interesting: E. pleasant   I. grave   S. boring

$$\underline{} \quad \underline{U} \quad \underline{} \quad \underline{L} \quad \underline{} \quad \underline{} \quad \underline{O} \quad \underline{} \quad \underline{} \quad \underline{} \quad \underline{} \quad \underline{} \quad \underline{}$$
   6   9   3   1   5   7   2   4   10   8

4.3 A Colonial First

The first town government in the 13 colonies was established in Massachusetts in 1633. In what town was this government established?

To answer the question, correct the sentences by replacing each underlined word with its antonym. Choose your answers from the words after each sentence. Write the letter of each answer in the space above its sentence number at the bottom of the page.

1. My mother always says to be <u>rude</u> and helpful to others.
   M. stern   H. polite   R. fresh

2. Pulling the child out of the way of the speeding car was a <u>timid</u> act.
   A. humorous   U. foolish   E. brave

3. Alex likes science and feels it is the most <u>boring</u> subject.
   S. interesting   N. confusing   P. dull

4. Strong winds will <u>gather</u> leaves in the yard.
   A. destroy   O. scatter   Y. reject

5. A major earthquake can <u>create</u> an entire city.
   I. build   H. refuse   E. destroy

6. The family picnic was <u>unpleasant</u> and everyone had a great time.
   S. interesting   R. delightful   N. nonsense

7. The brothers <u>refuse</u> to share the TV.
   R. agree   S. reject   D. gather

8. The knights pledged <u>treachery</u> to their king.
   C. loyalty   T. disloyalty   M. nonsense

9. The <u>sense</u> of poems like limericks is amusing.
   B. interesting   D. silliness   S. delight

10. Maria smiled as she read her little brother's <u>grave</u> story.
    I. unpleasant   C. boring   T. humorous

___ ___ ___ ___ ___ ___ ___ ___ ___ ___
 9   4   6   8   1   5   3   10   2   7

Homographs, I

Homographs are words that have the same spelling but different meanings. They have different origins, too. Some homographs also have different pronunciations.

1. yard (n): the area around a house

   yard (n): 36 inches

2. close (klōs) (adj): near

   close (klōz) (v): to shut

3. desert (dez´ ərt) (n): dry, barren land

   desert (di zûrt´) (v): to go away from

4. bear (n): a large mammal

   bear (v): to support or carry

5. pitcher (n): a position on a baseball team

   pitcher (n): a container for pouring liquid

6. pupil (n): a student

   pupil (n): the dark opening in the center of the eye

7. ball (n): a round object

   ball (n): a formal dance

8. count (n): a nobleman

   count (v): to name numbers in order

9. wind (wĭnd) (n): moving air

   wind (wīnd) (v): to turn

10. school (n): a place for learning

    school (n): a large group of fish

Vocabulary Tip

Homographs that have different pronunciations are also known as heteronyms.

5.1 A Lethal Creature

This small amphibian lives in the rain forests of Colombia, a country in South America. It is extremely poisonous. What is the name of this animal?

To answer the question, match each definition on the left with the correct homograph on the right. Write the letter of the homograph in the space above its definition number at the bottom of the page. Some letters are provided.

Definitions

1. a nobleman _____

2. a group of fish _____

3. dry, barren land _____

4. to carry; to support _____

5. the area around a house _____

6. to turn _____

7. a formal dance _____

8. a student _____

9. to shut _____

10. a container for pouring liquid _____

Homographs

D. desert

G. pitcher

A. count

O. pupil

S. yard

P. bear

R. close

N. wind

E. school

F. ball

```
__   __   L    __   __   __        __   __   I    __   __   __
10    8        3    2    6          4    8         5    8    6


__   __   __   T         __   __   __   __
 3    1    9              7    9    8   10
```

5.2 Hungry Elephants

Elephants are big animals. They are also big eaters. About how much time per day does an elephant spend eating?

To answer the question, read each sentence below. Match the underlined word with its definition. Choose your answers from the definitions after the sentences. Not all of the definitions will be used. Write the letter of each answer in the space above its sentence number at the bottom of the page. You will need to divide the letters into words.

1. The bear searched for food at the picnic grounds.

2. Lisa had to count the scissors to make sure all had been returned.

3. The raccoon mother did not desert her young during the terrible storm.

4. Teresa missed the bus and was late for school.

5. Jamal is a pitcher for his baseball team.

6. Please close the door.

7. The students learned about the role of the pupil in seeing.

8. Roberto pulled up the collar of his jacket to block the cold wind.

9. Cinderella lost her slipper at the ball.

10. The poster paper was a yard wide and four feet long.

Answers

M. area around a house	R. a baseball player
E. a formal dance	K. to turn
O. a large mammal	J. near
H. a part of the eye	G. 36 inches
W. to support; to carry	B. a group of fish
P. dry, barren land	I. to shut
S. to go away from	T. to name numbers in order
C. a student	L. a round object
U. moving air	V. a container for pouring liquid
A. a nobleman	N. a place for learning

___ ___ ___ ___ ___ ___ ___ ___ ___ ___ ___ ___ ___
 9   6   10   7   2   9   9   4   7   1   8   5   3

5.3 Sleepy Mammals

Some mammals sleep more than others. Three of the sleepiest spend about 80 percent of their lives dozing or sleeping. What are these sleepyhead mammals?

To answer the question, complete each sentence with the best word. Choose your answers from the words after the sentences. Write the letter of each answer in the space above its sentence number at the bottom of the page. Some letters are provided.

1. Mrs. Carter introduced the new _____ to the class.

2. Be sure to _____ your change after paying for something.

3. Taryn's favorite subject in _____ is math.

4. The _____ climbed the tree to get the honey in the beehive.

5. A _____ is a barren land that gets little rain.

6. We live _____ to the ocean and can smell the salty air.

7. The powerful _____ toppled a tree near our house.

8. Todd threw the _____ to his younger brother.

9. Her mother made a _____ of ice tea for Jenna and her friends.

10. A fence encloses our _____.

Answers

R. count	P. desert
L. wind	D. school
A. yard	M. bear
S. pitcher	I. pupil
H. close	O. ball

```
__  __  __  T   __  __    __  __  __  __  __  U   __  __
 9   7   8       6   9     8   5   8   9   9       4   9

__  __  __  __  __  __  __  __  __  __
10   2   4  10   3   1   7   7   8   9
```

Homographs, II

Homographs are words that have the same spelling but different meanings. They have different origins, too. Some homographs also have different pronunciations.

1. tire (n): rubber placed around a wheel

   tire (v): to become weary

2. rash (n): a sore on the skin

   rash (adj): hasty

3. root (n): the underground part of a plant

   root (v): to cheer for a person or team

4. tear (tēr) (n): a drop of liquid from the eye

   tear (tĕr) (v): to pull apart; to rip into pieces

5. duck (n): a water bird with webbed feet and a broad beak

   duck (v): to dip or dodge quickly

6. kind (n): same type

   kind (adj): friendly; helpful

7. brush (n): a tool for sweeping, cleaning, or painting

   brush (n): bushes

8. prune (n): a partially dried plum

   prune (v): to trim

9. present (prĕz´ ənt) (n): a gift

   present (prĕz´ ənt) (n): now; currently

   present (prĭ zĕnt) (v): to introduce

10. swallow (n): a small bird

    swallow (v): to take food in through the mouth

Vocabulary Tip

Many words in English have multiple meanings.

Homographs, II

6.1 Digesting Food

Digestion is the process of turning food into a form the body can use. All the foods we eat are digested. About how long does it take for a human being to digest a meal?

To answer the question, match each definition on the left with the correct homograph on the right. Write the letter of the homograph in the space above its definition number at the bottom of the page. You will need to reverse the order of the letters and then divide them into words. One letter is provided.

Definitions

1. a tool for cleaning, sweeping, or painting _____

2. a gift _____

3. to pull apart _____

4. a partially dried plum _____

5. to become weary _____

6. a sore on the skin _____

7. a small bird _____

8. same type _____

9. to dip or dodge quickly _____

10. to cheer for someone _____

Homographs

E. tear

T. swallow

S. duck

L. present

O. brush

U. kind

W. root

H. prune

V. tire

R. rash

$\frac{\quad}{9}$ $\frac{\quad}{6}$ $\frac{\quad}{8}$ $\frac{\quad}{1}$ $\frac{\quad}{4}$ $\frac{E}{\quad}$ $\frac{\quad}{5}$ $\frac{\quad}{2}$ $\frac{\quad}{3}$ $\frac{\quad}{10}$ $\frac{\quad}{7}$

6.2 A Radio First

In 1923, this president was the first to have his State of the Union address broadcast on the radio. Who was he?

To answer the question, read each sentence below. Match the underlined word with its definition. Choose your answers from the definitions after the sentences. Not all of the definitions will be used. Write the letter of each answer in the space above its sentence number at the bottom of the page. You will need to divide the letters into words.

1. Mr. Harris will <u>present</u> the members of the safety patrol at the assembly.

2. Dad and I cleared away the <u>brush</u> before planting the flowers.

3. A <u>root</u> of the big tree grew under the sidewalk and cracked the cement.

4. Justin could not ride his bike because of a flat <u>tire</u>.

5. My mother always tells us to chew and <u>swallow</u> our food slowly.

6. Ricky helped his brother <u>prune</u> the dead branches from the rosebush.

7. A <u>duck</u> may be awkward on land, but it moves easily in water.

8. I laughed so hard that a <u>tear</u> slipped from my eye.

9. Mae is impatient and sometimes makes <u>rash</u> decisions.

10. Mrs. Sanchez is a <u>kind</u> person and is always willing to help others.

Answers

S. now
L. to trim
R. to become weary
N. bushes
D. to introduce
U. a tool for sweeping
J. a small bird
Z. dip quickly
M. to cheer for someone
G. hasty

C. friendly, helpful
H. partially dried plum
P. same type
W. a sore on the skin
A. underground part of a plant
V. a water bird with webbed feet
E. to take in through the mouth
I. rubber placed around a wheel
O. a drop of liquid from the eye

___ ___ ___ ___ ___ ___ ___ ___ ___ ___ ___ ___ ___
10   3   6   7   4   2   10   8   8   6   4   1   9   5

6.3 New World Explorer

In 1524, this man was the first European to lead an expedition to reach what is now known as New York Harbor. Who was he?

To answer the question, complete each sentence with the correct word. Choose your answers from the words after the sentences. Write the letter of each answer in the space above its sentence number at the bottom of the page.

1. The mother _____, followed by her young, waddled to the pond.

2. The little boy quickly ripped off the wrapping paper of his birthday _____.

3. After driving over the nail, Mr. Evans had to buy a new _____.

4. Will's grandfather, an expert on birds, pointed to the _____ on the branch.

5. I always _____ for our high school team.

6. One _____ of animals is mammals.

7. Eric used the fine-tipped _____ for writing his name on his painting.

8. Danielle's little sister described the _____ as a wrinkled plum.

9. Poison ivy causes some people to break out with a terrible _____.

10. Our dog likes to _____ apart any paper he finds on the floor.

Answers

R. rash   E. present
A. brush   V. kind
D. tire   N. tear
Z. duck   O. swallow
G. prune   I. root

___ ___ ___ ___ ___ ___ ___ ___   ___ ___   ___ ___ ___ ___ ___ ___ ___ ___ ___
8   5   4   6   7   10   10   5   3   7   6   2   9   9   7   1   7   10   4

Homophones, I

Homophones are words that sound alike but have different meanings and different spellings.

1. hole (n): an opening

   whole (adj): complete; entire

2. cell (n): basic unit of life

   sell (v): to exchange for money

3. right (adj): correct; proper

   write (v): to set down in words

4. vain (adj): excessively proud; self-important; conceited

   vein (n): blood vessel

5. loan (n): something borrowed

   lone (adj): single

6. passed (v): went by

   past (adj): previous; former; no longer current

7. hear (v): to listen

   here (adv): in this place

8. steal (v): to rob

   steel (n): strong metal

9. way (n): path; road; course

 weigh (v): to measure how heavy something is

10. meat (n): food from an animal

 meet (v): to come together; to encounter

Vocabulary Tip

Watch for homophones when proofreading your writing. Homophones are easily misused.

7.1 Your Skin

Your skin is an amazing organ. It is your largest organ and protects the inner parts of your body. It grows, stretches, and heals itself. It is even waterproof. About how much skin does the average adult have?

To answer the question, match each definition on the left with the correct homophone on the right. Write the letter of each answer in the space above its definition number at the bottom of the page. Not all answers will be used. You will need to divide the letters into words. One letter is provided.

Definitions

1. to measure how heavy _____
2. something borrowed _____
3. basic unit of life _____
4. to listen _____
5. correct; proper _____
6. went by _____
7. complete _____
8. to rob _____
9. excessively proud _____
10. to come together _____

Homophones

J. sell	S. cell
R. right	C. write
A. steal	V. steel
F. whole	M. hole
D. way	N. weigh
T. vain	H. vein
I. meat	E. meet
W. passed	O. past
L. lone	Q. loan
P. here	Y. hear

__ __ __ __ __ __ __ __   U   __ __ __ __ __ __ __
9   6   10   1   9   4   3   2   8   5   10   7   10   10   9

© Gary Robert Muschla

7.2 An Early Writer of Horror

This author wrote about vampires in the nineteenth century. He wrote a story about Count Dracula, one of the most famous vampires of all. Who was this author?

To answer the question, read each sentence below. Find the definition of each underlined word. Choose your answers from the words after each sentence. Write the letter of each answer in the space above its sentence number at the bottom of the page.

1. The chipmunk ran down the <u>hole</u> under the rosebush.
   O. opening   U. door   A. complete

2. Marianna hoped to <u>sell</u> her old bike.
   R. unit of life   T. give away   E. exchange for money

3. Please put the books <u>here</u>.
   O. to listen   A. in this spot   I. in the next room

4. The frames of great buildings are made of <u>steel</u>.
   D. to rob   R. strong metal   S. wood and plastic

5. Aunt Joan is a vegetarian and does not eat <u>meat</u>.
   B. come together   C. interesting   T. food from animals

6. History is the study of <u>past</u> events.
   B. previous   T. future   C. interesting

7. The <u>lone</u> eagle flew over the river.
   P. flock   K. single   D. sharp-eyed

8. We checked the map to find the shortest <u>way</u> to the stadium.
   S. bus   N. schedule   M. course

9. Juan was lucky he did not cut a <u>vein</u> on his hand in his accident.
   S. blood vessel   P. section of skin   T. muscle

10. Always <u>write</u> your name on all of your papers.
    A. complete   I. spell   R. set down in words

   __   __   __   __   __   __   __   __   __   __
    6   10   3   8   9   5   1   7   2   4

7.3 Volcanoes

These scientists study volcanoes. What are they called?

    To answer the question, read each sentence below. If the underlined word is used correctly, write the letter for *correct* in the space above the sentence number at the bottom of the page. If the underlined word is not used correctly, write the letter for *incorrect*.

1. Sam finished the <u>whole</u> project in three days.
      A. correct   I. incorrect

2. We decided to <u>meat</u> at the library after school.
      J. correct   G. incorrect

3. Melissa got every answer <u>right</u> on her math test.
      S. correct   E. incorrect

4. Can you <u>hear</u> the distant echo?
      C. correct   M. incorrect

5. A <u>vain</u> carries blood back to the heart.
      U. correct   I. incorrect

6. On our <u>way</u> home from school, Mom took me to the mall.
      N. correct   O. incorrect

7. My older brother tried to <u>cell</u> his car.
      S. correct   T. incorrect

8. I finally paid back the <u>lone</u> of $5 to my sister.
      E. correct   O. incorrect

9. We <u>passed</u> the Statue of Liberty during our visit to New York City.
      V. correct   S. incorrect

10. <u>Steal</u> is a very strong metal used in construction.
       I. correct   L. incorrect

___ ___ ___ ___ ___ ___ ___ ___ ___ ___ ___ ___ ___ ___
9   8   10   4   1   6   8   10   8   2   5   3   7   3

Homophones, II

Homophones are words that sound alike but have different meanings and different spellings.

1. role (n): a character's part in a play, movie, or TV show

   roll (v): to move by turning over and over

2. stake (n): a stick with a pointed end

   steak (n): a slice of meat or fish for cooking

3. brake (n): a device that slows a car, bike, or machine

   break (v): to come apart; to separate into pieces

4. grate (v): to make a harsh, grinding sound

   great (adj): very big in size or number

5. close (v): to shut

   clothes (n): clothing; articles of dress; garments

6. knight (n): a medieval warrior

   night (n): the time between sunset and sunrise

7. pair (n): set of two; two that go together

   pear (n): a sweet, juicy fruit

8. waist (n): the part of the body between the ribs and hips

   waste (v): to make poor use of; to spend foolishly

9. scene (n): the place where something happens; a setting

   seen (v): viewed

10. colonel (n): an army officer with the rank just lower than a general

    kernel (n): a grain or seed

Vocabulary Tip

Computer spell-check programs do not always identify incorrectly used homophones.

Homophones, II

8.1 A High Point

At 19,340 feet (5,895 meters) above sea level, this is the highest point in Africa. What is it?

To answer the question, match each definition on the left with the correct homophone on the right. Write the letter of each answer in the space above its definition number at the bottom of the page. Not all answers will be used. One letter is provided.

Definitions

1. a medieval warrior _____

2. to come apart _____

3. a setting _____

4. garments _____

5. a stick with a pointed end _____

6. a character's part in a play _____

7. to make a harsh, grinding sound _____

8. a grain or seed _____

9. a set of two _____

10. to make poor use of _____

Homophones

K. clothes	C. close
N. role	B. roll
S. colonel	I. kernel
T. waste	E. waist
W. brake	A. break
D. great	O. grate
M. pair	Y. pear
Q. seen	U. scene
F. steak	R. stake
L. knight	P. night

__ __ __ __ __   __ __ __ __ __ __ __   J__ __ __
9 7 3 6 10   4 8 1 8 9 2 6   2 5 7

8.2 An Unusual Plant

This plant is found in the American Southwest. It can live for up to 200 years and can grow to be as tall as a five-story building. What is it?

To answer the question, complete each sentence with the correct homophone. Choose your answers from the words after each sentence. Write the letter of each answer in the space above its sentence number at the bottom of the page. Some letters are provided.

1. Natalie's Uncle John has the rank of _____ in the army.
   N. kernel   C. colonel

2. Jessie hurried to _____ the window to keep out the rain.
   R. close   E. clothes

3. Hailey knew the ending of the movie because she had _____ it before.
   G. seen   D. scene

4. The _____ storm brought heavy rain and strong winds.
   E. grate   U. great

5. Carl ordered _____, potato, and salad for dinner.
   O. stake   A. steak

6. Nicole taught her dog to sit and _____ over.
   D. role   T. roll

7. Stacey studied an hour after dinner last _____ for her science test.
   O. night   S. knight

8. Tyrell's father helped him repair the _____ on his bike.
   N. break   S. brake

9. Trisha ate a _____ for a snack after school.
   S. pear   R. pair

10. After playing football, Anthony noticed a bruise on his _____.
    C. waist   F. waste

```
__   A   __   U   __   __   __        __   A   __   __   __   __
 9       3        5    2    7         10        1    6    4    8
```

Homophones, II

8.3 After the Presidency

This president is the only man to serve in the House of Representatives after being president. Who was he?

To answer the question, read each sentence below. If the underlined word is used correctly, write the letter for *correct* in the space above the sentence number at the bottom of the page. If the underlined word is not used correctly, write the letter for *incorrect*. You will need to divide the letters into words. Some letters are provided.

1. Lauren's closet is full of <u>close</u>.
   A. correct   U. incorrect

2. The <u>night</u> rode off to save the princess.
   O. correct   M. incorrect

3. People should never <u>waist</u> food.
   H. correct   O. incorrect

4. Dad grilled a big <u>steak</u> for dinner.
   Y. correct   R. incorrect

5. Vanessa had the lead <u>role</u> in the school play.
   N. correct   O. incorrect

6. A <u>grate</u> crowd attended the president's speech.
   N. correct   S. incorrect

7. Tyler and his father planted a <u>pear</u> tree in the backyard.
   Q. correct   A. incorrect

8. The police quickly arrived on the <u>scene</u> of the accident.
   H. correct   O. incorrect

9. <u>Colonel</u> Smith had served in the army for 30 years.
   J. correct   T. incorrect

10. Dropping a dish may <u>brake</u> it.
    I. correct   A. incorrect

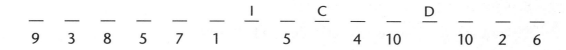

$\underline{\hspace{0.8em}}$ $\underline{\hspace{0.8em}}$ $\underline{\hspace{0.8em}}$ $\underline{\hspace{0.8em}}$ $\underline{\hspace{0.8em}}$ $\underline{\hspace{0.8em}}$ $\underline{\text{I}}$ $\underline{\hspace{0.8em}}$ $\underline{\text{C}}$ $\underline{\hspace{0.8em}}$ $\underline{\hspace{0.8em}}$ $\underline{\text{D}}$ $\underline{\hspace{0.8em}}$ $\underline{\hspace{0.8em}}$ $\underline{\hspace{0.8em}}$

  9   3   8   5   7   1   5   4   10   10   2   6

Homophones, II

Easily Confused Words, I

Some words have similar sounds or spellings but different meanings. These words are easily confused.

1. country (n): a nation

   county (n): a part of a state in the United States

2. later (adj): coming after the proper time

   latter (adj): the second of two

3. than (conj): used as a conjunction, *than* compares things

   then (adv): at that time

4. recent (adj): not long ago

   resent (v): to feel offended

5. dairy (n): a place where milk is produced or processed

   diary (n): a written record of what the writer has experienced

6. accept (n): to take something offered; to agree to

   except (prep): leaving out; not including

7. breath (n): air taken into the lungs

   breathe (v): to inhale and exhale

8. lightening (v): making less heavy

   lightning (n): static electrical discharge in the air

9. desert (n): a dry wasteland

    dessert (n): a tasty, usually sweet, food served at the end of a meal

10. coma (n): an unconscious state

    comma (n): a punctuation mark that separates words or ideas

Vocabulary Tip

Writers must work hard to avoid making mistakes with "easily confused words."

9.1 Alaska's State Flag

In 1927, a 13-year-old boy designed the state flag of Alaska. Who was he?
   To answer the question, match each definition with its word. Choose your answers from the words that follow each definition. Write the letter of each answer in the space above its definition number at the bottom of the page. One letter is provided.

1. at that time
   Y. then   R. than

2. a place where milk is produced or processed
   P. diary   B. dairy

3. a tasty, usually sweet, food served at the end of a meal
   E. dessert   A. desert

4. to inhale and exhale
   E. breathe   O. breath

5. a part of a state in the United States
   R. country   N. county

6. the second of two
   M. later   N. latter

7. to take something offered
   E. except   O. accept

8. static electrical discharge in the air
   B. lightning   T. lightening

9. a punctuation mark that separates words or ideas
   R. coma   S. comma

10. to feel offended
   N. resent   D. recent

___ ___ ___ ___ ___   ___ ___ N̲ ___ ___ ___
 8   3   10 6   1   2   4   9   7   5

9.2 Voyage to India

During the years 1497–1499, this explorer led a voyage to India. He and his men became the first Europeans to reach India by sailing around Africa's Cape of Good Hope. Who was he?

To answer the question, complete each sentence with the correct word. Choose your answers from the words after each sentence. Write the letter of each answer in the space above its sentence number at the bottom of the page. One letter is provided.

1. Russia is the largest _____ in the world.
   O. country   S. county

2. Tamara writes in her _____ every day.
   D. diary   V. dairy

3. Mr. Williams assigned all the problems on the page _____ number 12.
   I. accept   A. except

4. Martin's favorite _____ is ice cream.
   A. dessert   E. desert

5. The _____ storms have ended the drought.
   C. recent   T. resent

6. _____ your knapsack will make it easier to carry.
   E. Lightning   A. Lightening

7. Jason used a _____ to separate a list of words in a sentence.
   M. coma   V. comma

8. The Pacific Ocean is larger _____ the Atlantic Ocean.
   G. than   J. then

9. After running up the big hill, Jared was out of _____.
   D. breathe   M. breath

10. We decided to go to the mall _____.
    L. latter   S. later

__ _A_ __ __ __   __ __   __ __ __ __
 7   10   5   1   2   4   8   3   9   6

Easily Confused Words, I

45

9.3 Over the Atlantic

Charles Lindbergh was the first man to fly solo across the Atlantic Ocean in 1927. The first woman flew solo across the Atlantic in 1932. Who was she?

To answer the question, read each sentence below. If the underlined word is used correctly, write the letter for *correct* in the space above the sentence number at the bottom of the page. If the underlined word is not used correctly, write the letter for *incorrect*. Some letters are provided.

1. When we <u>breath</u>, we inhale and exhale air.
   R. correct   E. incorrect

2. <u>Lightening</u> always comes before thunder.
   Y. correct   I. incorrect

3. The fifth-graders visited a <u>dairy</u> for their class trip.
   T. correct   N. incorrect

4. Gina enjoys math more <u>then</u> reading.
   O. correct   E. incorrect

5. Our <u>country</u> is the biggest in our state.
   E. correct   H. incorrect

6. Survival is difficult in the <u>desert</u>.
   L. correct   H. incorrect

7. After the terrible accident, the driver of the car was in a <u>coma</u>.
   R. correct   U. incorrect

8. Mr. Wallace spoke to the students about <u>recent</u> problems at the bus stop.
   M. correct   E. incorrect

9. Because of the bad weather, their plane arrived <u>latter</u> than expected.
   S. correct   A. incorrect

10. In his haste not to miss the bus, Bradley packed everything <u>except</u> his lunch.
    R. correct   M. incorrect

$$\frac{\quad}{9} \quad \frac{\quad}{8} \quad \frac{\quad}{4} \quad \frac{\quad}{6} \quad \frac{\quad}{2} \quad \frac{A}{\quad} \qquad \frac{\quad}{1} \quad \frac{A}{\quad} \quad \frac{\quad}{10} \quad \frac{\quad}{5} \quad \frac{A}{\quad} \quad \frac{\quad}{7} \quad \frac{\quad}{3}$$

Easily Confused Words, I

Easily Confused Words, II

Some words have similar sounds or spellings but different meanings. These words are easily confused.

1. human (adj): of or relating to a person

   humane (adj): kind

2. loose (adj): not tight

   lose (v): to misplace; to be unable to find; to fail to win

3. expect (v): to look for a thing to happen

   suspect (n): a person thought to have committed a crime; (v): to mistrust

4. farther (adv): at or to a greater distance

   further (adv): to a greater extent; more

5. adapt (v): to adjust to new conditions

   adopt (v): to take into one's own family by choice

6. advice (n): a suggestion

   advise (v): to give advice

7. angel (n): a spiritual being

   angle (n): a figure formed by two lines that meet at a point

8. alley (n): a narrow street

   ally (n): a supporter; friend

9. wear (v): to carry or have on, for example, clothing

   were (v): a form of the verb *be*; existed

10. quiet (adj): silent; having little noise; calm

    quit (v): to stop

    quite (adv): completely; entirely; really

Vocabulary Tip

Keeping a list of words you find confusing can help you remember them.

10.1 Signer of the Constitution and President

Of the 39 men who signed the Constitution, only two went on to become president. One was George Washington. Who was the other?

To answer the question, match each definition with its word. Choose your answers from the words that follow each definition. Write the letter of each answer in the space above its definition number at the bottom of the page. You will need to divide the letters into words. Some letters are provided.

1. a suggestion
   I. advise   O. advice

2. more; to a greater extent
   S. further   T. farther

3. having little noise
   J. quit   M. quite   E. quiet

4. a spiritual being
   F. angle   M. angel

5. to misplace
   M. lose   N. loose

6. a supporter
   J. ally   T. alley

7. to adjust to new conditions
   K. adopt   D. adapt

8. a form of the verb *be*; existed
   I. were   O. wear

9. to mistrust
   S. expect   N. suspect

10. of or relating to a person
    A. human   O. humane

__ __ __ __ S̲ __ A̲ __ __ __ __ __
6   10 5   3   4   7   8   2   1   9

10.2 Early Astronomer

About 400 years ago, this Italian scientist developed telescopes. He used his telescopes to discover sunspots, mountains and valleys on the moon, and Jupiter's four biggest moons. Who was he?

To answer the question, complete each sentence with the correct word. Choose your answers from the words after each sentence. Write the letter of each answer in the space above its sentence number at the bottom of the page. Some letters are provided.

1. Whenever I have a problem, I ask my dad for _____.
   E. advise   A. advice

2. Taylor plans to _____ a puppy tomorrow.
   O. adapt   A. adopt

3. The bicycle shop was located at the end of the _____.
   I. alley   O. ally

4. Aunt Clair found the band to be _____ loud.
   E. quit   A. quiet   I. quite

5. Bekka used a ruler to draw an _____ for her math homework.
   L. angle   T. angel

6. The gate was crooked because the hinge was _____.
   S. lose   O. loose

7. Tamryn will _____ her new sweater to school today.
   G. wear   N. were

8. There have been no _____ announcements about the class trip.
   S. farther   L. further

9. I _____ Aunt Emma to arrive by noon.
   G. expect   N. suspect

10. People should always treat animals in a _____ manner.
    A. human   E. humane

```
__  __  __   I   L   __  __    __  __   L   __  __   E   __
 9   2   5           10   6     7   1        4   8        3
```

10.3 Two States

These were the last two states admitted to the United States. What states are they?

To answer the question, read each sentence below. If the underlined word is used correctly, write the letter for *correct* in the space above the sentence number at the bottom of the page. If the underlined word is not used correctly, write the letter for *incorrect*. You will need to divide the letters into words. Some letters are provided.

1. My mom can <u>advice</u> us what to do next on our project.
   O. correct   A. incorrect

2. Tim is my friend and <u>alley</u>.
   I. correct   A. incorrect

3. I won't <u>quit</u> until I solve this problem.
   I. correct   F. incorrect

4. A soft bed and lots of love will help a puppy <u>adopt</u> to his new home.
   O. correct   K. incorrect

5. James can throw a baseball <u>further</u> than his brother Jon.
   E. correct   I. incorrect

6. Brittany's mother warned her not to <u>lose</u> her key.
   L. correct   S. incorrect

7. Ali did not <u>expect</u> his surprise birthday party.
   S. correct   G. incorrect

8. The wooden beam had to be set at the proper <u>angel</u>.
   C. correct   H. incorrect

9. Jill and her mom <u>were</u> going to the mall.
   A. correct   E. incorrect

10. The creature that stepped off the spaceship had <u>human</u> characteristics.
    W. correct   L. incorrect

___   A   ___   ___   ___   ___   ___   ___   A   ___   ___   ___
8   10   2   3   5   1   6   7   4   9

Easily Confused Words, III

Some words have similar sounds or spellings but different meanings. These words are easily confused.

1. medal (n): an award

   metal (n): a substance such as iron, copper, or gold

2. set (v): to place or put something somewhere

   sit (v): to be in an upright position resting on the buttocks; for example, "sitting" in a chair

3. costume (n): clothing worn to imitate a person or animal

   custom (n): a usual action; a long-established habit

4. pastor (n): a minister

   pasture (n): a grassy field used by grazing animals

5. finale (n): the end

   finally (adv): at last; at the end

6. envelop (v): to surround

   envelope (n): paper cover for a letter or other materials

7. thorough (adj): complete; careful and exact

   through (prep): from beginning to end

8. certain (adj): confident; sure

   curtain (n): cloth hung at windows or in doors; a hanging screen on a stage

9. decent (adj): proper; right

   descent (n): the act of coming down

10. command (n): an order; (v): to give an order

    commend (v): to praise

Vocabulary Tip

When speaking or writing, always pay close attention to easily confused words.

11.1 Trail Marker

Pioneers traveling westward on the Oregon Trail through Nebraska used a natural land feature as a trail marker. It marked the end of the Nebraskan plains. What is the name of this land feature?

To answer the question, match each definition with its word. Choose your answers from the words that follow each definition. Write the letter of each answer in the space above its definition number at the bottom of the page. You will need to divide the letters into words.

1. to give an order
   E. command   O. commend

2. at last
   U. finale   I. finally

3. a grassy field used by cattle for grazing
   O. pasture   V. pastor

4. proper; right
   Y. decent   C. descent

5. clothing worn to imitate a person or animal
   O. custom   H. costume

6. complete
   K. thorough   S. through

7. cloth hung at windows or doors
   L. certain   N. curtain

8. to place or put something somewhere
   M. sit   C. set

9. to surround
   R. envelop   D. envelope

10. a substance such as iron, copper, or gold
    N. medal   M. metal

___ ___ ___ ___ ___ ___ ___ ___ ___ ___ ___
 8   5   2   10   7   1   4   9   3   8   6

Easily Confused Words, III

54

11.2 Doing Without Water

This little animal lives in the desert in North America. It can live its entire life without drinking water. It obtains enough water from seeds that it eats. Although it is only a few inches long, its large hind legs help it to jump 9 feet (2.75 meters). What is this animal called?

To answer the question, complete each sentence with the correct word. Choose your answers from the words after each sentence. Write the letter of each answer in the space above its sentence number at the bottom of the page. You will need to divide the letters into words. One letter is provided.

1. Lauren helped her little brother _____ in the chair at the table.
   A. sit   E. set

2. The fog seemed to _____ the entire town.
   A. envelop   U. envelope

3. Each member of the basketball team received a _____ for winning the championship.
   O. metal   A. medal

4. We drove _____ the Lincoln Tunnel on our trip to New York City.
   N. thorough   R. through

5. The plane's _____ during the storm was a little scary.
   R. descent   H. decent

6. Deena's _____ was voted the most original at the Halloween party.
   M. custom   G. costume

7. Evan and his grandfather led the cows to the _____.
   T. pasture   S. pastor

8. Mrs. Wilson, our principal, will _____ students for their excellent behavior.
   I. command   N. commend

9. Shari was _____ she had handed in her book report on time.
   W. curtain   K. certain

10. The audience stood and applauded at the play's _____.
    O. finale   A. finally

```
__   __   __   __   __   __        O    __   __   __   __
 9    3    8    6    2    4              10    5    1    7
```

11.3 Space Pioneer

In 1926, this man launched the first liquid fuel space rocket. He is sometimes called the Father of Space Flight. What was his name?

To answer the question, read each sentence below. If the underlined word is used correctly, write the letter for *correct* in the space above the sentence number at the bottom of the page. If the underlined word is not used correctly, write the letter for *incorrect*. Some letters are provided.

1. Melanie wondered what was inside the big <u>envelop</u> that had her name on it.
   E. correct   A. incorrect

2. The teacher instructed the class to be <u>thorough</u> with their research.
   O. correct   I. incorrect

3. David and his father <u>set</u> in front-row seats at the game.
   W. correct   R. incorrect

4. Claudia was impatient for the <u>curtain</u> to rise and the play to start.
   G. correct   M. incorrect

5. <u>Pastor</u> Smith gave the sermon at church on Sunday.
   D. correct   T. incorrect

6. The statue in the town square was made of <u>medal</u>.
   L. correct   R. incorrect

7. Rodney was glad when the long drive was <u>finale</u> done.
   O. correct   E. incorrect

8. Kelli gave her dog a <u>command</u> to roll over.
   D. correct   S. incorrect

9. The hawk's <u>decent</u> was swift and smooth.
   N. correct   B. incorrect

10. Taking your shoes off when entering the house is a <u>custom</u> in Japan.
    T. correct   D. incorrect

_	O	_	_	_	_		_	_	_	D	_	R	_
3	9	7	6	10		4	2	5		1		8

Words with Latin Roots, I

Many English words have Latin roots. Some of these roots can be traced back to Latin that was spoken thousands of years ago. Some Latin roots (with their meanings in parentheses) are *act* (do), *form* (shape), *terr* (land), *port* (carry), and *loc* (place).

1. action (n): the process of doing something; act; deed

   Martin's quick <u>action</u> saved Jason from tripping.

2. porter (n): a person who carries luggage

   The <u>porter</u> placed our luggage in our car.

3. uniform (n): clothes worn by members of a group or team

   Sara picked up her soccer <u>uniform</u> yesterday.

4. actor (n): a person who plays a character in a story; a performer

   Nathan was an <u>actor</u> in the school play.

5. locate (v): to find

   Kyle used a map to <u>locate</u> the museum.

6. transport (v): to carry from one place to another

   The moving company will <u>transport</u> our furniture to our new house.

7. territory (n): land; an area that a government exercises authority over

   The pioneers settled new <u>territory</u>.

8. report (n): a detailed account; (v): to give an account

   Marissa wrote a <u>report</u> about Canada.

   The committee will <u>report</u> its findings today.

9. transform (v): to change in form, appearance, or nature

   By building dams, beavers can <u>transform</u> streams and creeks.

10. react (v): to act back; to respond

    Some dogs <u>react</u> to loud sirens by howling.

Vocabulary Tip

Understanding the roots of words can help you understand their meanings.

Words with Latin Roots, I

12.1 To the South Pole

In 1911, this Norwegian explorer led the first expedition to reach the South Pole. Who was he?

To answer the question, complete each sentence with the correct word. Choose your answers from the words after the sentences. Write the letter of each answer in the space above its sentence number at the bottom of the page.

1. Marci chose *Charlotte's Web* for her book _____.

2. I tried to _____ Walt Disney World on a map of Florida.

3. Joshua enjoys stage plays and hopes to be an _____ someday.

4. Trains _____ materials, products, and people.

5. At Gabriella's school, every student wears a _____.

6. The exciting movie had lots of _____.

7. Much _____ in the southwestern part of the United States is desert.

8. The evil magician can _____ himself into a dragon.

9. Cats often _____ with curiosity to something new.

10. A _____ took our suitcases into the hotel for us.

Answers

R. react
O. actor
M. uniform
U. locate
E. territory

A. porter
N. transform
L. report
D. action
S. transport

— — — — —   — — — — — — — — —
9 3 10 1 6   10 5 2 8 6 4 7 8

12.2 First to Secede

In 1860, this state was the first to secede (break away) from the United States. Other Southern states followed, and by the next year the Civil War had begun. What state was the first to secede?

To answer the question, match each word on the right with its definition on the left. Write the letter of each answer in the space above its definition number at the bottom of the page. You will need to divide the letters into words. One letter is provided.

Definitions   **Words**

1. to give an account _____   C. territory

2. the process of doing something _____   N. porter

3. to find _____   A. actor

4. clothes worn by the members of a group or team _____ S. transport

5. a person who carries luggage _____   L. react

6. to change in form, appearance, or nature _____   U. locate

7. to act back _____   H. report

8. a person who plays a character in a story _____   T. transform

9. to carry from one place to another _____   O. uniform

10. land that a government exercises authority over _____ I. action

__ __ __ __ __ __ __ **R** __ __ __ __ __
9   4   3   6   1   10   8   4   7   2   5   8

12.3 Volleyball

William G. Morgan invented the game of volleyball in 1895. But the game was not originally called volleyball. What was volleyball originally called?

To answer the question, read each sentence below. Find the word or phrase that has the closest meaning to the underlined word or phrase. Choose your answers from the words or phrases that follow each sentence. Write the letter of each answer in the space above its sentence number at the bottom of the page.

1. Most puppies <u>react</u> quickly to the sound of their name.
   E. forget   T. respond   R. play

2. Jason is <u>an actor</u> in a local play.
   E. a director   I. a musician   T. a performer

3. Buses <u>carry</u> children to and from school in many towns and cities.
   N. transport   D. send   R. provide

4. Treasure hunters try to <u>locate</u> lost wealth.
   E. search for   A. spend   I. find

5. Mr. Baxter's charitable <u>action</u> provided the library with a hundred new books.
   O. answer   E. deed   S. phone call

6. We waited for a <u>person</u> to help us with our luggage.
   H. waiter   D. guide   O. porter

7. The <u>territory</u> beyond the mountains was perfect for farming.
   T. land   J. weather   C. place

8. The police chief will give his <u>report</u> about crime to the mayor tonight.
   S. speech   R. ideas   M. account

9. The wizard hoped to <u>transform</u> lead into gold.
   U. make   E. change   O. melt

10. Alyssa's father must wear <u>special clothing</u> for his job.
    R. hats   N. a uniform   T. a badge

___ ___ ___ ___ ___ ___ ___ ___ ___ ___
8   4   10   1   6   3   9   7   2   5

Words with Latin Roots, I

Words with Latin Roots, II

Many English words have Latin roots. Some of these roots can be traced back to Latin that was spoken thousands of years ago. Some Latin roots (with their meanings in parentheses) are *aqua* (water), *cam* (field), *corp* (body), *pop* (people), and *tain* (hold).

1. population (n): the number of people living in a place

   The <u>population</u> of New York City is about eight and a half million.

2. aquarium (n): a tank for fish

   We have an <u>aquarium</u> in our classroom.

3. contain (v): to have; to hold; to include

   Science books usually <u>contain</u> a glossary.

4. corporation (n): a business; a company

   General Motors is a large <u>corporation</u>.

5. popular (adj): well liked

   Chad is a <u>popular</u> student.

6. aqueduct (n): a pipe or channel for carrying water from one place to another

   An <u>aqueduct</u> brings water from a lake to our town.

7. campus (n): the grounds of a school or college

   The high school's <u>campus</u> includes a football field, a baseball field, and a track.

8. corps (n): a group of people with special training who act together

   Uncle Bill is a member of a drum and bugle <u>corps</u>.

9. camper (n): a person who lives outdoors for a time, often in a tent

   The <u>camper</u> set his tent on a field.

10. aquatic (adj): relating to the water

    Fish are <u>aquatic</u> animals.

Vocabulary Tip

Words with the same Latin roots have related meanings.

13.1 A Space Term

Astronomers have special names for objects in space. What term do they use for large objects such as stars and planets?

To answer the question, find the word for each definition. Choose your answers from the words after each definition. Write the letter of each answer in the space above its definition number at the bottom of the page. You will need to divide the letters into words. One letter is provided.

1. a pipe or channel for carrying water from one place to another
   C. aquarium   S. aqueduct   M. aquatic

2. a person who lives outdoors for a time, usually in a tent
   I. camper   A. settler   E. campus

3. to have, hold, or include
   U. maintain   O. contain   T. order

4. the number of people living in a place
   O. persons   E. popular   A. population

5. the grounds of a school or college
   B. campus   E. area   R. camp

6. a tank for fish
   I. aquatic   U. aqua   E. aquarium

7. well liked
   Y. popular   N. good   S. enjoy

8. a business; a company
   H. corps   S. campus   C. corporation

9. relating to water
   D. aquatic   E. aquarium   T. aqueduct

10. a group of people with special training who act together
    V. population   L. corps   A. corporation

__	__	__	__	__	T	__	__	__	__	__	__	__
8	6	10	6	1		2	4	10	5	3	9	7

13.2 Explorer and Captain

In the years 1487–1488, a Portuguese sea captain led the first European expedition to sail around the southern tip of Africa. This opened a sea route to Asia. What was the captain's name?

To answer the question, complete each sentence with the correct word. Choose your answers from the words after the sentences. Write the letter of each answer in the space above its sentence number at the bottom of the page. Some letters are provided.

1. Dogs and cats are _____ pets in America.

2. Dad and I bought fish for our _____.

3. Anna's mother works for a large _____.

4. An _____ provides the city with water.

5. A _____ is a person who enjoys living outdoors.

6. Monica belongs to an environmental youth _____ that helps keep parks clean.

7. The college my sister goes to has a beautiful _____.

8. The boxes in the attic _____ old clothes.

9. China has the largest _____ of any country in the world.

10. Dari loves the water and enjoys _____ sports.

Answers

I. aquarium	R. corps
S. camper	A. contain
M. aqueduct	U. popular
O. campus	D. aquatic
B. population	T. corporation

_	_	_	_		H	_		L	_	_		E	_		_	_	_	_
9	8	6	3		7			7	4			1			10	2	8	5

13.3 A Milestone Amendment

In 1920, passage of this amendment to the US Constitution gave women the right to vote. What amendment was this?

To answer the question, find the word or phrase that best defines each word below. Choose your answers from the words or phrases that follow each word. Write the letter of each answer in the space above the word's number at the bottom of the page. You will need to reverse the order of the letters.

1. population: I. citizens   N. people   E. home owners

2. corporation: T. company   N. charity   V. organize

3. aqueduct: U. water   T. relating to water   E. channel for water

4. camper: E. campsite   T. outdoors person   O. hunter

5. aquarium: O. pool   W. schools of fish   I. fish tank

6. campus: T. playground   D. campsite   H. grounds around school

7. corps: U. corporation   E. company   N. specially trained group

8. aquatic: E. relating to water   L. sea life   N. water sports

9. contain: T. a box   N. to hold   F. package

10. popular: E. well liked   T. enjoyable   N. friendly

___ ___ ___ ___ ___ ___ ___ ___ ___ ___
6   4   1   10   3   2   8   7   5   9

Words with Greek Roots, I

Many English words have Greek roots. The origins of many of these words can be traced back thousands of years. Some Greek roots (with their meanings in parentheses) are *auto* (self), *bio* (life), *cycl* (circle), *geo* (earth), *graph* (write), and *photo* (light).

1. autograph (n): a person's signature

   People waited in line for the movie star's <u>autograph</u>.

2. geography (n): the study of the earth's surface

   <u>Geography</u> is Marianna's favorite subject because she likes learning about the earth's land features.

3. photograph (n): a picture taken by a camera

   Mom keeps a <u>photograph</u> of our family on her desk.

4. autobiography (n): a written account of a person's life, written by the person

   The singer's <u>autobiography</u> told of his hard work to become a star.

5. cycle (n): a regularly repeated event or series of events

   Caitlyn's class learned about the life <u>cycle</u> of frogs.

6. geometry (n): the study of points, lines, angles, figures, and measurement

   Larissa got an A on her test in <u>geometry</u>.

7. telephoto (adj): pertaining to a lens that allows a camera to take pictures at great distances

   The photographer used a <u>telephoto</u> lens to take pictures of the lion.

8. cyclone (n): a powerful storm with whirling winds; a tornado

   The <u>cyclone</u> caused great destruction over the countryside.

9. recycle (v): to repeat a cycle

   We <u>recycle</u> newspapers, bottles, and aluminum cans every week.

10. biography (n): a written account of a person's life, written by another person

    William enjoyed reading the <u>biography</u> of Thomas Jefferson.

Vocabulary Tip

Understanding Greek roots can help you understand the meanings of many modern English words.

14.1 Our National Anthem

"The Star-Spangled Banner" is our national anthem. This person wrote the poem that became the lyrics of "The Star-Spangled Banner." Who was he?

To answer the question, find the word for each definition. Choose your answers from the words after each definition. Write the letter of each answer in the space above its definition number at the bottom of the page. You will need to divide the letters into words. Some letters are provided.

1. pertaining to a lens that allows a camera to take pictures at great distances
   N. telephoto   C. telephone   R. photographic

2. a written account of a person's life, written by the person
   I. autograph   E. biography   A. autobiography

3. a powerful storm with whirling winds
   O. cycle   U. downpour   E. cyclone

4. the study of points, lines, angles, figures, and measurement
   K. geography   C. geometry   H. mathematics

5. a written account of a person's life, written by another person
   T. biography   M. autobiography   D. autograph

6. to repeat a cycle
   O. redo   H. create   R. recycle

7. a person's signature
   K. autograph   C. autobiography   A. biography

8. a picture taken by a camera
   I. autobiography   S. photograph   C. telephoto

9. a regularly repeated event
   T. recycle   D. action   F. cycle

10. the study of the earth's surface
    E. geometry   Y. geography   I. biography

__ __ __ __ __ I__ __ __ __ O__ __ __ __ __ __
9   6   2   1   4   8 8   4   5   5   7   3 10

14.2 The Five Senses

You gain information about the world around you through your senses. You have five main senses. What are they?

To answer the question, complete each sentence with the correct word. Choose your answers from the words after the sentences. Write the letter of each answer in the space above its sentence number at the bottom of the page. You will need to divide the letters into words. Some letters are provided.

1. Her assignment for _____ required Tess to measure angles with a protractor.

2. Daniel needed a _____ lens to take pictures of the faraway mountains.

3. When we _____ materials, we reduce waste.

4. We are studying _____ and learning about the continents.

5. The governor wrote about his entire life in his _____.

6. The changing seasons are an example of a _____.

7. The old _____ showed the bridge being built.

8. A _____ is a very destructive storm.

9. Julie hoped to get the author's _____ at the book signing.

10. For his report about Abraham Lincoln, Vincent read a _____ of Lincoln.

Answers

E. geography
T. cycle
L. autograph
A. geometry
H. recycle

U. telephoto
C. biography
I. autobiography
S. photograph
G. cyclone

Words with Greek Roots, I

14.3 Shadow on the Earth

When the moon passes between the earth and the sun, the moon casts a shadow on the earth. What is this event called?

To answer the question, read each sentence below. If the underlined word is used correctly, write the letter for *correct* in the space above the sentence number at the bottom of the page. If the underlined word is not used correctly, write the letter for *incorrect*. Some letters are provided.

1. To help conserve resources, we <u>cycle</u> as much as we can.
   I. correct   E. incorrect

2. In an <u>autobiography</u>, the author writes about someone else's life.
   N. correct   R. incorrect

3. The mountain peaks in the <u>photograph</u> were beautiful.
   S. correct   E. incorrect

4. LuAnn learned about the earth's land forms in <u>geometry</u>.
   A. correct   O. incorrect

5. Brian used a <u>telephoto</u> lens to take a picture of the eagle in the distance.
   I. correct   E. incorrect

6. Rebecca enjoys <u>geography</u> because she likes learning about the earth's surface.
   L. correct   R. incorrect

7. A <u>cycle</u> does not repeat.
   K. correct   C. incorrect

8. The author wrote his own <u>biography</u>.
   C. correct   S. incorrect

9. At the game, Crystal got the <u>autograph</u> of her favorite player.
   P. correct   M. incorrect

10. The <u>cyclone</u> brought heavy rain but no wind.
    E. correct   A. incorrect

Words with Greek Roots, I

__ __ __ __ __   __ __ L̲ __ __ __ E̲
 8   4   6 10   2   1   7   5   9   3

© Gary Robert Muschla

71

Words with Greek Roots, II

Many English words have Greek roots. The origins of some of these words can be traced back thousands of years. Some Greek roots (with their meanings in parentheses) are *gram* (letter, written), *log* (word), *meter* (measure), *arch* (ruler, leader), *phon* (sound), and *sci* (know).

1. monarch (n): the ruler of a nation; a king or queen

   The <u>monarch</u> was known for her wisdom and was loved by her people.

2. grammar (n): the study of the forms and uses of words in sentences

   <u>Grammar</u> is an important part of language arts.

3. thermometer (n): an instrument used for measuring temperature

   Heather checked the <u>thermometer</u> outside to find how cold it was.

4. science (n): knowledge based on observed facts, experimentation, and organized information

   Through <u>science</u> we can understand the world around us.

5. diagram (n): a drawing that shows how something works

   Mr. Ross showed the class a <u>diagram</u> of the inside of the space station.

6. barometer (n): an instrument used for measuring air pressure

   A low reading on a <u>barometer</u> usually means a storm is coming.

7. prologue (n): an introduction or opening to a story

   The book began with a <u>prologue</u>.

8. diameter (n): a line segment passing through the center of a circle with its endpoints on the circle

   Kevin measured the <u>diameter</u> of the circle with his ruler.

9. apology (n): words saying that a person is sorry

   Please accept my <u>apology</u> for coming to the meeting late.

10. matriarch (n): a woman who rules or leads a family or clan

    Angela's grandmother is the <u>matriarch</u> of her family.

Vocabulary Tip

Words with the same Greek roots have related meanings.

Words with Greek Roots, II

15.1 A Not Very Smart Dinosaur

A certain dinosaur had a brain about the size of a walnut. But this dinosaur weighed about 6,000 pounds (2,722 kilograms). What was the name of this dinosaur?

To answer the question, find the word for each definition. Choose your answers from the words after each definition. Write the letter of each answer in the space above its definition number at the bottom of the page. One letter is provided.

1. words saying a person is sorry
   H. greeting   S. apology   N. prologue

2. knowledge based on observed facts, experimentation, and organized information
   S. science   B. geography   A. grammar

3. a drawing that shows how something works
   A. barometer   E. diagram   O. diameter

4. a woman who rules or leads a family or clan
   A. monarch   O. princess   U. matriarch

5. a line passing through the center of a circle with its endpoints on the circle
   N. diagram   T. barometer   O. diameter

6. the study of the forms and uses of words in sentences
   E. language   U. grammar   A. diagram

7. an introduction or opening to a story
   A. prologue   U. diagram   I. diameter

8. an instrument used for measuring temperature
   R. barometer   T. thermometer   L. science

9. a king or queen
   U. matriarch   S. diameter   R. monarch

10. an instrument used for measuring air pressure
    G. barometer   N. thermometer   L. diameter

__	__	__	__	__	S	__	__	__	__	__
2	8	3	10	5		7	4	9	6	1

15.2 Cat Lovers

Cats are popular pets in the United States. A special word describes people who love cats. What is a person who loves cats called?

To answer the question, complete each sentence with the correct word. Choose your answers from the words after the sentences. Write the letter of each answer in the space above its sentence number at the bottom of the page.

1. The wise old woman was the _____ of the family.

2. Sonya wrote a _____ for her story.

3. Justin measured the _____ of the circle.

4. Kristin offered an _____ for causing the argument.

5. The _____ showed the life cycle of a butterfly.

6. Paulo enjoys _____ because he likes to experiment with things.

7. Scientists use a _____ to measure air pressure.

8. To speak and write clearly, a person must understand _____.

9. The temperature on the _____ was 55 degrees.

10. The brave _____ led his men into battle.

Answers

L. thermometer   H. apology
I. prologue   P. barometer
A. grammar   U. matriarch
O. diameter   E. diagram
R. monarch   N. science

__	__		__	__	__	__	__	__	__	__	__	__
8	6		8	2	9	1	10	3	7	4	2	9	5

15.3 Tiny Blood Vessels

Arteries are blood vessels that carry blood away from your heart. Veins are blood vessels that carry blood back to your heart. Tiny blood vessels connect arteries to veins. What are these tiny blood vessels called?

To answer the question, read each sentence below. If the underlined word is used correctly, write the letter for *correct* in the space above the sentence number at the bottom of the page. If the underlined word is not used correctly, write the letter for *incorrect*. One letter is provided.

1. The <u>prologue</u> was an interesting start to the novel.
   I. correct   A. incorrect

2. The king was the <u>matriarch</u> of his country.
   U. correct   I. incorrect

3. Of all the subjects in school, Kareem enjoys <u>science</u> the most.
   L. correct   A. incorrect

4. Natalie wrote an <u>apology</u> for not being able to attend her cousin's party.
   A. correct   O. incorrect

5. We checked the temperature on the <u>barometer</u>.
   U. correct   E. incorrect

6. The queen was a great <u>monarch</u> who ruled her people wisely.
   L. correct   R. incorrect

7. The <u>diameter</u> did not go through the center of the circle.
   H. correct   R. incorrect

8. Kyle used a <u>thermometer</u> to measure the speed of the wind.
   S. correct   C. incorrect

9. The <u>diagram</u> showed how the windmill created electricity.
   S. correct   N. incorrect

10. <u>Grammar</u> is an important topic in math.
    T. correct   P. incorrect

<u> </u> <u> </u> <u> </u> <u> </u> <u> </u> <u> </u> <u>A</u> <u> </u> <u> </u> <u> </u> <u> </u>

 8   4   10   1   6   3   7   2   5   9

Words with Greek Roots, II

Prefixes, I

A prefix is a word part added to the beginning of a word. A prefix changes the meaning of a word to which it is added. Following are some common prefixes and their meanings:

im-	not; without
mis-	bad; wrong
pre-	before
un-	not; opposite of
under-	below; less than

1. prehistoric (adj): at a time before written history

   <u>Prehistoric</u> cave paintings tell much about early humans.

2. misspell (v): to spell incorrectly

   Talia tries not to <u>misspell</u> any words when writing.

3. underground (adj): beneath the surface of the earth

   The <u>underground</u> water pipe was broken.

4. precaution (n): an action taken in advance, usually for safety; a safeguard

   As a <u>precaution</u>, we locked the car.

5. unsafe (adj): dangerous; risky

   The ice was <u>unsafe</u> for skating.

6. impossible (adj): not able to happen; unreal

   With our current technology, it is <u>impossible</u> for humans to visit Mars.

7. underline (v): to draw a line beneath

   The teacher instructed the class to <u>underline</u> new words.

8. misplace (v): to put in a wrong place; to lose

   I always <u>misplace</u> my pencil.

9. impolite (adj): showing bad manners; rude; discourteous

   Speaking with your mouth full of food is <u>impolite</u>.

10. unsure (adj): not certain; doubtful

    Kim was <u>unsure</u> of her answer.

Vocabulary Tip

The meaning of a prefix is a clue to a word's meaning.

16.1 The Man Who Named the Dinosaurs

This English scientist was the first to use the term *dinosaur*, meaning "terrible lizard." Who was he?

To answer the question, find the word or phrase that best defines each word below. Choose your answers from the words or phrases after each word. Write the letter of each answer in the space above the word's number at the bottom of the page.

1. precaution: I. careless   E. safeguard   U. unreal

2. impolite: H. rude   M. unhappy   L. mistaken

3. unsure: A. correct   I. not certain   O. certain

4. impossible: E. easy   U. believable   O. not able to happen

5. unsafe: A. dangerous   I. careful   Y. possible

6. misspell: S. missing letter   N. spell incorrectly D. make a correction

7. underground: D. a cellar   U. far below   R. beneath earth's surface

8. misplace: W. to lose   L. to find   T. to put away

9. underline: S. make a drawing   D. to draw a line beneath   M. to highlight

10. prehistoric: L. early history   O. before people   C. before written history

___ ___ ___ ___ ___ ___ ___   ___ ___ ___ ___
 7   3   10   2   5   7   9   4   8   1   6

16.2 The Powerful Heart

Your heart pumps blood through your body. It never rests. About how many times does the average human heart beat each day?

To answer the question, complete each sentence with the correct word. Choose your answers from the words after the sentences. Write the letter of each answer in the space above its sentence number at the bottom of the page. You will need to divide the letters into words.

1. When not at home in the evening, we leave the lights on as a _____.

2. It is _____ to see bacteria without a microscope.

3. Interrupting people when they are speaking is _____.

4. Archeologists found ancient pottery and stone tools at the site of the

   _____ village.

5. Jessica was _____ where she had left her math book.

6. The teacher cautioned her students not to _____ any words on their stories.

7. It is helpful to _____ important words in your notes.

8. Riding a bicycle without a helmet is _____.

9. Many animals live in _____ nests and dens for protection against predators.

10. I am very organized and hardly ever _____ anything.

Answers

E. unsure   U. precaution
D. underline   T. misspell
R. prehistoric   A. impolite
S. unsafe   N. misplace
H. impossible   O. underground

— — — — — — — — — — — — — — — — — — —
9 10 5 2 1 10 7 4 5 7 6 2 9 1 8 3 10 7

16.3 A Bright Idea

In 1929, Sam Foster introduced a new product to America. Today there are many types of this product, and they are found just about everywhere. What are they?

To answer the question, read each sentence below. Replace the underlined word or phrase with the word or phrase that has a similar meaning. Choose your answers from the words after each sentence. Write the letter of each answer in the space above its sentence number at the bottom of the page.

1. It is <u>unsafe</u> to swim at a beach without lifeguards.
   U. fun   E. unwise   A. dangerous

2. People who talk during a movie are <u>showing bad manners</u>.
   I. friendly   U. impolite   A. talkative

3. Jordan was <u>unsure</u> her project would win a prize at the science exhibit.
   U. positive   N. hopeful   S. doubtful

4. The <u>advance action</u> we took limited damage from the storm.
   G. precaution   M. activity   C. ideas

5. It is easy to <u>spell words incorrectly</u> when you write quickly.
   U. misuse words   M. make mistakes   E. misspell

6. The spear tips in the cave were <u>from a time before written history</u>.
   N. prehistoric   I. old   R. puzzling

7. Many things that were <u>not able to happen</u> a few years ago are common today.
   L. planned   S. impossible   B. started

8. The cable was laid <u>beneath the lawn</u>.
   T. low   M. covered   S. underground

9. Be sure to <u>draw a line beneath</u> the title of the poster.
   S. underline   N. color   D. highlight

10. Our dog and cat <u>misplace</u> their toys all the time.
    N. discover   L. lose   T. hide

$$\overline{}\quad \overline{}\quad \overline{}\quad \overline{}\quad \overline{}\quad \overline{}\quad \overline{}\quad \overline{}\quad \overline{}\quad \overline{}$$

   8   2   6   4   10   1   7   3   5   9

Prefixes, II

A prefix is a word part added to the beginning of a word. A prefix changes the meaning of a word to which it is added. Following are some common prefixes and their meanings:

dis-	not; opposite of
re-	again
tele-	distant
sub-	under; below
non-	not; opposite of

1. rewrite (v): to write again, especially to improve writing; to revise

   Brittany must <u>rewrite</u> her story.

2. dishonest (adj): untrustworthy; deceitful

   Cheating is a <u>dishonest</u> act.

3. subzero (adj): below zero

   The cold temperature was <u>subzero</u>.

4. dislike (v): to have a bad feeling for; to object to; to disapprove of

   I <u>dislike</u> the shorter hours of daylight during the winter.

5. nonstop (adj): having made no pauses or breaks; (adv): done without a stop

   Darius and his family took a <u>nonstop</u> flight to California.

   We worked <u>nonstop</u> on our project yesterday after school.

6. renew (v): to make new again; to restore

   Melissa must <u>renew</u> a magazine subscription.

7. telephone (n): a device for speaking over long distances

   I enjoy talking to my friends on the <u>telephone</u>.

8. disagree (v): to differ in opinion; to oppose

   Although Jon and James are twins, they <u>disagree</u> on almost everything.

9. telescope (n): an instrument for seeing distant objects, especially in space

   A <u>telescope</u> is an important tool of astronomers.

10. nonfat (adj): containing no fat, especially in foods with the fat removed

    We drink <u>nonfat</u> milk in our family.

Vocabulary Tip

Prefixes are always added in front of a base word or root.

Prefixes, II

17.1 A Grand Biome

A biome is a large region of the earth. The environment of a biome results from its geographical features and climate. Many scientists believe that a certain biome is home to about half of the world's plants and animals. What biome is this?

To answer the question, match each word on the left with its definition on the right. Write the letter of each answer in the space above the word's number at the bottom of the page. You will need to divide the letters into words. One letter is provided.

Prefixes, II

Words	Definitions
1. nonstop _____	N. untrustworthy
2. telescope _____	A. below zero
3. dishonest _____	I. instrument for seeing distant objects
4. renew _____	O. having made no pauses or breaks
5. subzero _____	H. having the fat removed
6. disagree _____	F. to disapprove of
7. nonfat _____	R. to revise
8. telephone _____	S. to differ in opinion
9. dislike _____	E. to restore
10. rewrite _____	T. device for speaking over long distances

T __ __ __ __ __ __ __ __ __ __ __ __
   7   4 10 5 2 3 9 1 10 4 6 8

17.2 A Bird Group Name

Most people know the group names of many common animals. For example, a group of deer is known as a herd. A group of chickens is a flock. A group of dogs is a pack. What group of birds is a "bellowing"?

To answer the question, complete each sentence with the correct word. Choose your answers from the words after the sentences. Write the letter of each answer in the space above its sentence number at the bottom of the page.

1. Evie looked through the _____ and saw mountains and craters on the moon.

2. Our dogs hate getting wet and _____ baths.

3. Every January, Sal must _____ the license for his dog.

4. I had to _____ my story three times before I was satisfied with it.

5. The new puppy cried _____ his first night in his new home.

6. Paul and his brother _____ about politics and support different candidates.

7. It is hard to trust _____ people.

8. Each week we talk on the _____ with my grandmother who lives in Arizona.

9. I shiver just thinking about _____ temperatures.

10. _____ foods are a part of a healthy diet.

Answers

S. subzero
F. dishonest
H. nonstop
L. telephone
I. telescope

N. nonfat
B. rewrite
C. dislike
U. disagree
E. renew

__	__	__	__	__	__	__	__	__	__	__
4	6	8	8	7	1	10	2	5	3	9

17.3 A Famous Animator

Although this man did not create the first animated cartoon, he made many animated films. He is responsible for many animated characters known the world over. Who was he?

To answer the question, read each sentence below. If the underlined word is used correctly, write the letter for *correct* in the space above its sentence number at the bottom of the page. If the underlined word is not used correctly, write the letter for *incorrect*. You will need to divide the letters into words.

1. My mother has to <u>renew</u> her driver's license every four years.
   I. correct   U. incorrect

2. I <u>dislike</u> heights because I am afraid of falling.
   N. correct   L. incorrect

3. We took several breaks on our <u>nonstop</u> drive to the city.
   O. correct   A. incorrect

4. A <u>telescope</u> is useful for viewing tiny objects that are very close.
   I. correct   E. incorrect

5. A <u>dishonest</u> person always tells the truth.
   H. correct   L. incorrect

6. A <u>telephone</u> makes it possible for people who are apart to talk to each other.
   T. correct   N. incorrect

7. <u>Nonfat</u> foods have high amounts of fat.
   S. correct   Y. incorrect

8. The cold wave brought <u>subzero</u> temperatures to much of the country.
   D. correct   M. incorrect

9. They <u>disagree</u> on everything and share the same opinions.
   J. correct   W. incorrect

10. Sean decided to <u>rewrite</u> the opening of his story once more.
    S. correct   C. incorrect

—	—	—	—	—	—	—	—	—	—
9	3	5	6	8	1	10	2	4	7

Suffixes, I

A suffix is a word part added to the end of a base word or root. A suffix adds to the meaning of the word. Following are some common suffixes and their meanings:

-able	able to; can be
-ful	full of
-less	without
-er; -or	one who
-ship	state or quality of

1. thoughtful (adj): engaged in thinking; serious; being considerate of others

   Uncle Thomas is a <u>thoughtful</u> man who is always willing to help others.

2. teacher (n): one who provides knowledge to others; instructor; educator

   Mrs. Parker is Rogelio's favorite <u>teacher</u>.

3. remarkable (adj): noteworthy; outstanding; very special

   The championship game was <u>remarkable</u>.

4. penmanship (n): the skill, style, or manner of handwriting

   Alyssa has very neat <u>penmanship</u>.

5. careless (adj): not cautious; reckless; sloppy

   The <u>careless</u> child knocked the cookie jar off the table.

6. doctor (n): a person trained to practice medicine; physician

   The <u>doctor</u> said that Lara had a cold.

7. hardship (n): trouble; misfortune; difficulty

   The storm caused <u>hardship</u> for travelers.

8. careful (adj): cautious; attentive; alert

   You should always be <u>careful</u> when crossing a street.

9. inventor (n): one who makes something never made before; creator; developer

   Thomas Edison, who developed the lightbulb, was a great <u>inventor</u>.

10. comfortable (adj): restful; contented; relaxed

    The new couch was very <u>comfortable</u>.

Vocabulary Tip

Understanding the meanings of suffixes can help you understand the meanings of words.

Suffixes, I

18.1 Peanuts

This scientist developed more than 300 uses for peanuts. Who was he?

To answer the question, find the word or phrase that has a similar meaning to each word below. Choose your answers from the words or phrases after each word. Write the letter of each answer in the space above the word's number at the bottom of the page. Some letters are provided.

1. hardship: N. cautious   C. misfortune   R. restful

2. inventor: O. creator   A. educator   U. doctor

3. penmanship: N. very special   R. one who teaches   V. manner of
                                                               handwriting

4. thoughtful: I. one who makes   E. physician   S. engaged in
                                                               thinking

5. comfortable: R. restful   T. alert   M. outstanding

6. teacher: H. physician   N. instructor   T. reckless

7. remarkable: E. attentive   I. outstanding   O. serious

8. careful: U. difficult   Y. relaxed   A. cautious

9. doctor: W. creator   J. inventor   G. physician

10. careless: E. reckless   I. contented   U. noteworthy

— — — — — —   W — _ H — — — T — —
9 10 2 5 9 10   8 4   7 6 9   2 6

— — — — — —
1 8 5 3 10 5

18.2 Revolutionary Sea Captain

Born in Scotland, this man became a captain in the American fleet during the Revolutionary War. He won many battles. After the war, he was the only naval officer to be given a gold medal by Congress. Who was he?

To answer the question, complete each sentence with the correct word. Choose your answers from the words after the sentences. Write the letter of each answer in the space above its sentence number at the bottom of the page. You will need to divide the letters into words.

1. Try not to make _____ mistakes in your work.

2. Our _____ does not give homework for the weekend.

3. George Eastman was the _____ of the first handheld camera.

4. Pioneers suffered great _____ on their journey westward.

5. You must be _____ when walking on icy sidewalks.

6. Flying over the countryside in a hot-air balloon for the first time was a

   _____ experience.

7. Roberto forms his letters neatly and has excellent _____.

8. Marta listened to the question, organized her ideas, and gave a _____ answer.

9. The _____ prescribed medicine for Jason's sore throat.

10. Once we got settled, I was very _____ in our new home.

Answers

H. inventor
J. doctor
O. thoughtful
P. comfortable
S. remarkable

N. careful
E. teacher
A. careless
L. hardship
U. penmanship

___	___	___	___	___	___	___	___	___	___	___	___	___
9	8	3	5	10	1	7	4	9	8	5	2	6

Suffixes, I

18.3 A Fast Dinosaur

Scientists believe a certain dinosaur could run up to 40 miles per hour (64 kilometers per hour). This was the fastest of all dinosaurs. What dinosaur was this?

To answer the question, read each sentence below. Replace the underlined word or phrase with the word or phrase that has a similar meaning. Choose your answers from the words after each sentence. Write the letter of each answer in the space above its sentence number at the bottom of the page. Some letters are provided.

1. My instructor expects us to work hard in school.
   E. inventor   I. teacher   U. physician

2. The flood caused great hardship for many people.
   M. trouble   T. cautious   C. serious

3. Spaceflight is a noteworthy achievement for human beings.
   K. difficult   H. remarkable   N. reckless

4. George Crum was the creator of potato chips in 1853.
   R. attentive   P. noteworthy   M. inventor

5. You should go to a physician when you are ill.
   N. a doctor   S. an educator   G. an inventor

6. Lying in the hammock outside was restful.
   N. alert   O. trouble   S. comfortable

7. Peter's father taught him to be careful when using tools.
   O. cautious   A. serious   T. relaxed

8. Neat handwriting is a result of practice.
   E. contented   U. penmanship   I. outstanding

9. James is always considerate of others.
   L. special   R. cautious   T. thoughtful

10. Sloppy work usually leads to mistakes.
    R. careless   T. restful   N. outstanding

__	__	__	__	__	__	O	__	I	__	__	__
7	10	5	1	9	3	4		2	8	6	

Suffixes, I

Suffixes, II

A suffix is a word part added to the end of a base word or root. A suffix adds to the meaning of the word. Following are some common suffixes and their meanings:

-ous	full of
-ness	state of or quality of
-ish	relating to
-y	full of; state of
-ment	act of or state of

1. government (n): a system for ruling a nation, state, city, or town

   Our <u>government</u> protects the rights of its citizens.

2. childish (adj): behaving like a child; immature; silly

   Peter's <u>childish</u> behavior is not amusing.

3. kindness (n): friendly or helpful behavior; goodness

   Everyone respects Mr. Smith because of his <u>kindness</u>.

4. enormous (adj): very big; gigantic; huge

   The mountain was <u>enormous</u>.

5. sadness (n): sorrow; grief; unhappiness

   The movie's tragic ending filled me with <u>sadness</u>.

6. enjoyment (n): pleasure; satisfaction

   Tom's <u>enjoyment</u> of the game was capped by his team winning.

7. sunny (adj): bright with sunshine

   The day of our family picnic was warm and <u>sunny</u>.

8. selfish (adj): thinking of oneself; having no care for others

   The little girl was <u>selfish</u> and would not share her toys.

9. agreement (n): an understanding or arrangement between people

   The boys and girls reached an <u>agreement</u> to share the soccer field during recess.

10. joyous (n): very happy; cheerful; glad

    Having our lost dog returned to us made the day <u>joyous</u> for our family.

Vocabulary Tip

Some suffixes change a word's part of speech. For example, the suffix -ish added to the noun child makes the adjective childish.

19.1 Heading South

West Quoddy Head, Maine, is the easternmost point of the United States. The northernmost spot is Point Barrow, Alaska. The westernmost point is Cape Wrangell, Alaska. What is the southernmost point of the United States?

   To answer the question, find the word or phrase that has a similar meaning to each word below. Choose your answers from the words or phrases after each word. Write the letter of each answer in the space above the word's number at the bottom of the page. One letter is provided.

1. enormous: E. pleasure   A. gigantic   O. silly

2. sunny: I. satisfaction   E. friendly   A. bright with sunshine

3. agreement: A. argument   Y. happiness   E. an arrangement

4. kindness: A. goodness   O. silliness   U. gladness

5. enjoyment: K. pleasure   E. friendly behavior   L. understanding

6. selfish: E. satisfaction   N. very big   I. thinking of oneself

7. government: A. a company   H. system for ruling   F. president

8. sadness: L. gigantic   R. immature   W. sorrow

9. childish: I. silly   O. gladness   A. not caring

10. joyous: H. immature   M. risky   L. very happy

```
 __   __       __   __   __       __   __   __   A   __   __
 5    2        10   1    3        7    4    8        6    9
```

19.2 A Young Author

This author was only 15 years old when he wrote the original draft of *Eragon*. Who is he?

To answer the question, complete each sentence with the correct word. Choose your answers from the words after the sentences. Write the letter of each answer in the space above its sentence number at the bottom of the page. Some letters are provided.

1. The _____ of the wonderful night was shared by everyone.

2. The day was _____ with deep-blue skies.

3. The wedding was a _____ event for our family.

4. The president is the head of our _____.

5. We love winter and were filled with _____ when our snowman melted.

6. _____ people think of themselves first.

7. Everyone should treat others with _____ every day.

8. The skyscrapers of the city were _____.

9. The students were in _____ about the topic for their project.

10. Misbehaving in class is _____ behavior.

Answers

H. sunny	P. kindness
C. agreement	L. childish
E. enjoyment	R. sadness
I. enormous	T. selfish
O. joyous	N. government

__ __ __ __ S __   __ __ __ __ __ __   __ A __ __ __ __ __
9 2 5 8   6 3 7 2 1 5   7   3 10 8 4 8

19.3 Colony Founder

William Penn founded the colony of Pennsylvania in 1682. He also planned and named a city. What city was this?

To answer the question, read each sentence below. If the underlined word is used correctly, write the letter for *correct* in the space above its sentence number at the bottom of the page. If the underlined word is not used correctly, write the letter for *incorrect*. Some letters are provided.

1. The sky on the <u>sunny</u> day was filled with clouds.
   I. correct   E. incorrect

2. <u>Selfish</u> people are willing to share with others.
   U. correct   I. incorrect

3. Hurricanes are <u>enormous</u> storms that can cause much damage.
   I. correct   O. incorrect

4. <u>Sadness</u> does not mean sorrow.
   F. correct   L. incorrect

5. Jamie loves reading and finds great <u>enjoyment</u> in a good story.
   L. correct   H. incorrect

6. Everyone at the meeting was in <u>agreement</u> that a new school needed to be built.
   A. correct   S. incorrect

7. The birth of the baby was a <u>joyous</u> time for the family.
   H. correct   A. incorrect

8. To behave properly in school, students should act in a <u>childish</u> manner.
   N. correct   D. incorrect

9. The evil witch, with <u>kindness</u> in her heart, cast a terrible spell upon the village.
   W. correct   P. incorrect

10. A country's <u>government</u> is its system for ruling.
    H. correct   T. incorrect

__	__	__	__	A	__	__	__	P	__	__	__
9	7	3	5		8	1	4		10	2	6

Descriptive Words, I

Speakers and writers use descriptive words to add details to their ideas.

1. narrow (adj): not wide; thin

   We drove carefully down the <u>narrow</u> road.

2. famous (adj): well known; honored

   Lisa's aunt is a <u>famous</u> author.

3. slight (adj): small; minor; slender

   There is a <u>slight</u> chance for rain today.

4. towering (adj): very high; lofty; imposing

   The <u>towering</u> mountains reached high into the sky.

5. exquisite (adj): beautifully made; very lovely; delicate

   The flower vase was <u>exquisite</u>.

6. fantastic (adj): strange; odd; weird

   The story was set in a <u>fantastic</u> future.

7. different (adj): not alike; not like others; various

   The students were given <u>different</u> topics for their reports.

8. dense (adj): crowded together; thick

   The <u>dense</u> forest was filled with trees, vines, and bushes.

9. drowsy (adj): sleepy; half-asleep

   When it was time for his nap, the baby became <u>drowsy</u>.

10. expensive (adj): costly; high in price

   The movie star wore <u>expensive</u> clothing and jewelry.

> **Vocabulary Tip**
>
> **W**hen speaking or writing, choose descriptive words that paint pictures in the minds of listeners and readers.

20.1 Vermont

Vermont is a state in New England. There is something that all of the New England states except Vermont do. What is this?

To answer the question, match each word on the left with its definition on the right. Write the letter of each answer in the space above the word's number at the bottom of the page. You will need to divide the letters into words. Some letters are provided.

Words

1. towering _____

2. drowsy _____

3. narrow _____

4. exquisite _____

5. different _____

6. fantastic _____

7. famous _____

8. dense _____

9. slight _____

10. expensive _____

Definitions

C. not alike

D. sleepy

T. well known

A. thick

N. not wide

R. small

O. weird

E. costly

I. very high

B. very lovely

__ __ __ __ __ __ __ H̲ __
4   6   9   2   10 9   7   10

__ __ L̲ __ __ __ __ __ __ __ __ __
8   7   8   3   7   1   5   6   5   10 8   3

© Gary Robert Muschla

Descriptive Words, I

99

20.2 A First for the Colonies

The first of these was established in the colonies in Virginia in 1620. It was made possible by the donations of English landowners. What was it?

To answer the question, complete each sentence with the correct word. Choose your answers from the words after each sentence. Write the letter of each answer in the space above its sentence number at the bottom of the page. You will need to divide the letters into words. Some letters are provided.

1. I like science fiction stories with _____ creatures.
   U. expensive   O. narrow   I. fantastic

2. By the end of the long day, my little sister was tired and _____.
   C. drowsy   L. exquisite   W. famous

3. George Washington is one of America's most _____ leaders.
   E. unknown   A. famous   O. different

4. Only one person at a time could walk up the _____ stairway of the lighthouse.
   L. narrow   D. slight   M. dense

5. The _____ fog made it hard to see.
   N. slight   R. dense   E. fantastic

6. We saw many _____ exhibits at the museum.
   S. drowsy   M. narrow   L. different

7. According to the weather report, the possibility for snow today is _____.
   P. slight   H. expensive   A. dense

8. I was amazed at the city's _____ skyscrapers.
   A. slight   Y. towering   E. surprising

9. The tickets for the front-row seats at the concert were _____.
   C. narrow   R. expensive   N. thoughtful

10. The small, handmade ornaments were _____.
    B. exquisite   H. towering   S. dense

$$\underline{\hphantom{X}}\ \underline{U}\ \underline{\hphantom{X}}\ \underline{\hphantom{X}}\ \underline{I}\ \underline{\hphantom{X}}\ \underline{\hphantom{X}}\ \underline{\hphantom{X}}\ \underline{B}\ \underline{\hphantom{X}}\ \underline{\hphantom{X}}\ \underline{\hphantom{X}}\ \underline{\hphantom{X}}$$

7   10   4   2   6   1   9   3   5   8

20.3 Measuring the Clouds

This instrument is used to measure the height of clouds. What is it?

To answer the question, read each sentence below. Replace each underlined word or phrase with the word that has a similar meaning. Choose your answers from the words after each sentence. Write the letter of each answer in the space above its sentence number at the bottom of the page.

1. Norman Rockwell is a <u>well-known</u> American painter.
   E. famous   I. fantastic   O. different

2. Bryan had a <u>minor</u> cold, but he is better now.
   U. dense   O. slender   I. slight

3. The ice-cream shop had <u>various</u> flavors to choose from.
   E. expensive   O. different   A. delicate

4. Our vacation was <u>costly</u>, but we enjoyed every minute of it.
   I. fantastic   A. minor   E. expensive

5. The stream was shallow and <u>not wide</u>.
   E. narrow   O. harsh   Y. delicate

6. Even though I was <u>half-asleep</u>, I tried to stay awake to watch the end of the game.
   S. honored   L. drowsy   M. alert

7. Looking at the <u>thick</u> weeds, Tom wondered how he would ever clean out the flower bed.
   S. strange   N. harsh   R. dense

8. The flower pot was <u>beautifully made</u>.
   P. expensive   M. exquisite   H. weird

9. The <u>lofty</u> peaks of the mountain range were snow-capped.
   C. towering   A. various   L. narrow

10. Some people believe that <u>fantastic</u> beings from outer space have visited Earth.
    M. different   H. imposing   T. strange

__	__	__	__	__	__	__	__	__	__
9	5	2	6	3	8	1	10	4	7

Descriptive Words, I

Descriptive Words, II

Speakers and writers use descriptive words to add details to their ideas.

1. **primitive** (adj): uncivilized; undeveloped; early; original

   The explorers found the remains of a <u>primitive</u> village.

2. **eager** (adj): impatiently or excitedly wanting or waiting for something; enthusiastic

   Anna was <u>eager</u> for the soccer game to begin.

3. **unhappy** (adj): not happy; sad

   When the toy broke, the little boy was <u>unhappy</u>.

4. **weary** (adj): tired; exhausted; worn out

   We were <u>weary</u> from the long drive.

5. **excessive** (adj): extreme; too much

   Peter thought that the many rules in Mrs. Hart's class were <u>excessive</u>.

6. **pleasant** (adj): delightful; pleasing; agreeable; friendly

   The day of our class trip was sunny and <u>pleasant</u>.

7. **dazzling** (adj): brilliant; gleaming; splendid

   The ring was <u>dazzling</u> in the light.

8. **peaceful** (adj): calm; quiet; liking peace

   After the storm passed, we enjoyed a <u>peaceful</u> night.

9. frequent (adj): regular; usual; continual

Everyone in the family looked forward to Grandmother's <u>frequent</u> visits.

10. proud (adj): feeling pleased and satisfied

Angela was <u>proud</u> of her report card.

Vocabulary Tip

Descriptive words are also known as modifiers.

Descriptive Words, II

21.1 Colony for Religious Freedom

The colony of Rhode Island was founded in 1636. The colony was among the first colonies to guarantee religious freedom. Who was the founder of Rhode Island?

To answer the question, find the word or phrase that best defines each word below. Choose your answers from the choices after each word. Write the letter of each answer in the space above the word's number at the bottom of the page. You will need to divide the letters into words. Some letters are provided.

1. pleasant: M. exhausted   R. delightful   G. satisfied

2. eager: T. calm   S. liking peace   M. impatiently waiting

3. dazzling: S. honorable   N. tired   W. brilliant

4. proud: V. worn out   O. feeling satisfied   R. truthful

5. unhappy: A. sad   E. gleaming   H. quiet

6. weary: G. agreeable   K. entire   I. tired

7. primitive: G. uncivilized   W. not happy   M. feeling pleased

8. frequent: Y. splendid   L. regular   H. friendly

9. peaceful: N. exhausted   R. calm   W. firm

10. excessive: E. worn out   O. feeling satisfied   S. extreme

___ ___ ___ E   ___ ___ ___ L   ___ I   ___ ___ ___
 9   4   7   1   3   6   8   5   2   10

Descriptive Words, II

21.2 A Colonial Newspaper

The *Pennsylvania Gazette* at one time was the most popular newspaper in the American colonies. Who was its first publisher?

To answer the question, complete each sentence with the correct word. Choose your answers from the words after the sentences. Write the letter of each answer in the space above its sentence number at the bottom of the page. You will need to divide the letters into words. One letter is provided.

1. Receiving the safety patrol award made Carlos _____.

2. The fireworks were _____ in the night sky.

3. Natalie was _____ when she missed the party.

4. The _____ rainfall caused major flooding in the town.

5. After the very busy day, Thomas looked forward to a _____ evening at home.

6. To make sure we keep up with our work, Mr. Landis gives our class _____ quizzes.

7. Our dog is always _____ to play.

8. After hiking all day, we were _____.

9. Aunt Jane and I spent a _____ afternoon together shopping.

10. The _____ pottery was used by people who lived thousands of years ago.

Answers

E. peaceful   N. weary
F. primitive   I. unhappy
K. dazzling   L. frequent
J. eager   A. excessive
B. pleasant   R. proud

___ ___ ___ ___ ___ M ___ ___ ___ ___ ___ ___ ___ ___ ___
 9   5   8   7   4   3   8 10   1   4   8   2   6   3   8

21.3 The Tallest Dinosaur

Scientists believe that a certain type of dinosaur was the tallest, with a height measuring about 60 feet (18 meters). What dinosaur was this?

To answer the question, read each sentence below. Replace each underlined word or phrase with the word or phrase that has a similar meaning. Choose your answers from the words after each sentence. Write the letter of each answer in the space above its sentence number at the bottom of the page. Some letters are provided.

1. The hostess greeted us with a <u>friendly</u> smile.
   E. quiet   O. pleasant   I. tired

2. Kelly was <u>weary</u> after finishing her report.
   U. unhappy   R. honorable   O. exhausted

3. Because of his job, my father makes <u>regular</u> trips to Los Angeles.
   O. frequent   E. peaceful   A. splendid

4. The amount of snowfall in our town this year was <u>extreme</u>.
   L. weary   S. excessive   N. unhappy

5. The circus performers put on <u>a splendid</u> show.
   W. an honorable   R. a dazzling   O. a proud

6. The nights are <u>quiet</u> in the mountains.
   D. peaceful   T. brilliant   M. enthusiastic

7. Brendon was <u>feeling satisfied</u> that he had been named student of the month.
   O. quiet   A. proud   U. agreeable

8. <u>Uncivilized</u> humans created wonderful cave paintings.
   S. Eager   X. Unhappy   N. Primitive

9. Ali was <u>impatiently waiting</u> to get his turn at the game.
   S. eager   T. delightful   A. calm

10. Catching a cold always makes Jennifer _____.
    E. excessive   U. exhausted   I. unhappy

__	__	U	__	__	P	__	__	E	__	__	__	__
9	7		5	2		1	4		10	6	3	8

Descriptive Words, II

Descriptive Words, III

Speakers and writers use descriptive words to add details to their ideas.

1. mysterious (adj): hard to understand; puzzling

   The <u>mysterious</u> package turned out to be a gift from my grandmother.

2. peculiar (adj): odd; strange; curious

   The <u>peculiar</u> sound was coming from the attic.

3. frantic (adj): excited with fear; agitated; panicky

   I was <u>frantic</u> as I searched for my social studies report.

4. energetic (adj): very active; lively; vigorous

   Billy is <u>energetic</u> and never gets tired.

5. scarce (adj): hard to get; rare; uncommon

   Replacement parts for the old car were <u>scarce</u>.

6. generous (adj): unselfish; willing to share or give

   Mrs. Hollings made a <u>generous</u> donation to the library.

7. enough (adj): plenty; ample; sufficient

   Mom always brings more than <u>enough</u> food for the family picnic.

8. ancient (adj): very old; of a long time ago; primitive

   The <u>ancient</u> village offered details of how people lived thousands of years ago.

9. humble (adj): not proud; modest; not important

   Juan was <u>humble</u> in accepting his award for community service.

10. splendid (adj): wonderful; dazzling; magnificent

    The fifth-grade winter concert was a <u>splendid</u> event.

Vocabulary Tip

When speaking or writing, choose descriptive words carefully. Use those that provide sharp details.

22.1 An Animal Scientist

A zoologist is a person who studies animals. Zoologists who study certain kinds of animals have special names. What is a zoologist who specializes in studying reptiles and amphibians called?

To answer the question, match each word on the left with its definition on the right. Write the letter of each answer in the space above the word's number at the bottom of the page.

Words

1. generous _____
2. frantic _____
3. enough _____
4. energetic _____
5. humble _____
6. mysterious _____
7. splendid _____
8. peculiar _____
9. ancient _____
10. scarce _____

Definitions

S. very active

T. puzzling

H. strange

O. hard to get

L. panicky

E. modest

I. primitive

G. wonderful

P. unselfish

R. plenty

__ __ __ __ __ __ __ __ __ __ __ __ __
8   5   3   1   5   6   10 2   10 7   9   4   6

22.2 A Famous Author

Lemony Snicket is the author of the books in *A Series of Unfortunate Events*. What is Lemony Snicket's real name?

To answer the question, complete each sentence with the correct word. Choose your answers from the words after each sentence. Write the letter of each answer in the space above its sentence number at the bottom of the page. Some letters are provided.

1. The _____ stillness in the air made us think a storm was brewing.
   L. frantic   I. peculiar   O. splendid

2. I was certain I found an _____ arrowhead.
   D. ancient   W. enough   T. energetic

3. More people than expected came to the party, but we had _____ food.
   N. scarce   S. humble   R. enough

4. Our teacher is always _____ with her time and willing to help us.
   I. energetic   E. generous   A. splendid

5. The _____ sounds in the old house frightened me.
   S. scarce   M. ancient   H. mysterious

6. Babysitting the _____ child was exhausting.
   L. energetic   O. humble   R. generous

7. The circus performers put on a _____ show.
   R. humble   N. scarce   L. splendid

8. Fresh food and water were _____ the day after the destructive storm.
   R. mysterious   D. scarce   W. generous

9. Even though he has great wealth, Mr. Jones lives in a _____ house.
   A. humble   E. generous   O. frantic

10. Having overslept, I was _____ that I would miss the bus.
    L. scarce   N. frantic   S. energetic

```
__   A    __   __  __  __      __  __   N   __  __   E   __
8        10    1   4   7       5   9        2   6       3
```

22.3 A Deep Summertime Sleep

To survive winter in cold climates, some animals go into a state of inactivity. Their breathing and heart rates become very low. This state is called hibernation. In hot climates, some animals go into a state of inactivity to survive summer. What is this state called?

To answer the question, read each sentence below. Replace the underlined word with a word that has a similar meaning. Choose your answers from the words after each sentence. Write the letter of each answer in the space above its sentence number at the bottom of the page. One letter is provided.

1. All of the dancers enjoyed the energetic music.
   I. lively   E. wonderful   A. sufficient

2. Trees are uncommon at the peaks of high mountains.
   O. ample   A. scarce   U. vigorous

3. The mysterious scratching was caused by a cat.
   A. rare   T. magnificent   E. puzzling

4. Although she is a successful artist, Mrs. Ellis remains a humble person.
   C. wonderful   N. modest   R. lively

5. Rosa always gives to charity and is the most unselfish person I know.
   N. sufficient   A. generous   H. magnificent

6. We had no explanation for the odd lights in the night sky.
   G. scarce   M. agitated   V. peculiar

7. Five scoops of ice cream were sufficient even for me.
   I. enough   U. dazzling   A. vigorous

8. No one knew who built the primitive monument.
   E. modest   O. ancient   N. uncommon

9. Frantic people tried to leave the island before the hurricane arrived.
   L. Unselfish   D. Ample   T. Panicky

10. We spent a wonderful day sightseeing in the city.
    S. splendid   P. rare   M. damp

__	__	__	T	__	__	__	__	__	__	__
5	3	10		1	6	2	9	7	8	4

Descriptive Words, IV

Speakers and writers use descriptive words to add details to their ideas.

1. artificial (adj): man-made; synthetic; not natural

   The <u>artificial</u> flowers looked real.

2. spare (adj): extra; additional

   We always keep <u>spare</u> batteries on hand.

3. exotic (adj): unfamiliar; strange; unusual

   The parrot had <u>exotic</u> feathers.

4. difficult (adj): hard; demanding; burdensome

   Last night's math homework was <u>difficult</u>.

5. beautiful (adj): lovely; very pretty

   The sunset was <u>beautiful</u>.

6. ordinary (adj): common; usual; regular

   We enjoyed a quiet, <u>ordinary</u> day.

7. vigorous (adj): energetic; intense

   Our dance instructor led us through a <u>vigorous</u> workout.

8. impatient (adj): restless; not able to put up with delay

   Our flight was late, and we were <u>impatient</u> to get home.

9. spectacular (adj): marvelous; wonderful; breathtaking

   The singers at the concert put on a <u>spectacular</u> performance.

10. soggy (adj): soaked; thoroughly wet

    The ground was <u>soggy</u> after the heavy rain.

Vocabulary Tip

Most descriptive words are adjectives.

Descriptive Words, IV

23.1 Planet Sizes

Of the planets in our solar system, Earth is more than twice the size of the smallest. But the biggest planet in our solar system is more than ten times the size of Earth. What are the smallest planet and the biggest planet in our solar system?

To answer the question, match each word on the left with its definition on the right. Write the letter of each answer in the space above the word's number at the bottom of the page. You will need to divide the letters into words.

Words

1. impatient _____

2. beautiful _____

3. artificial _____

4. ordinary _____

5. soggy _____

6. vigorous _____

7. spare _____

8. difficult _____

9. exotic _____

10. spectacular _____

Definitions

R. soaked; thoroughly wet

T. energetic; intense

J. marvelous; wonderful; breathtaking

E. unfamiliar; strange; unusual

I. man-made; synthetic; not natural

P. hard; demanding; burdensome

U. restless; not able to put up with delay

C. extra; additional

M. lovely; very pretty

Y. common; usual; regular

___ ___ ___ ___ ___ ___ ___ ___ ___ ___ ___ ___ ___ ___
 2   9   5   7   1   5   4   10   1   8   3   6   9   5

23.2 States of Matter

Matter is anything that has mass and takes up space. Matter has three states. What are these three states?

To answer the question, read each sentence below. Replace each underlined word with the word that has a similar meaning. Choose your answers from the words after each sentence. Write the letter of each answer in the space above its sentence number at the bottom of the page. You will need to divide the letters into words. Some letters are provided.

1. Because of the broken water pipe, the rug was <u>soaked</u>.
   - T. artificial
   - M. exotic
   - D. soggy

2. Today's basketball practice was <u>intense</u>.
   - U. beautiful
   - I. vigorous
   - A. spectacular

3. I have the <u>usual</u> amount of homework tonight.
   - O. ordinary
   - A. difficult
   - I. spare

4. The robot's <u>synthetic</u> skin seemed lifelike.
   - U. artificial
   - A. beautiful
   - E. ordinary

5. The fireworks over the bay were <u>breathtaking</u>.
   - U. vigorous
   - S. impatient
   - L. spectacular

6. Kaylyn wore a <u>lovely</u> dress for wedding.
   - U. difficult
   - A. beautiful
   - E. vigorous

7. The zoo had <u>unusual</u> animals from around the world.
   - N. ordinary
   - L. exotic
   - R. artificial

8. Mom makes sure I have <u>extra</u> pens, pencils, and paper for school.
   - G. spectacular
   - Q. spare
   - M. exotic

9. Because of the snowstorm, traveling was <u>hard</u> for everyone.
   - S. difficult
   - P. beautiful
   - E. soggy

10. James is <u>restless</u> and does not like to wait.
   - M. vigorous
   - T. difficult
   - G. impatient

_	I	_	_	I	_	_	_	S	_	_	_	_	D
5	8	4		1	10	6		9	3	7	2		

23.3 Falling Water

When clouds have too much moisture, water falls to the earth. Depending upon the temperatures in the clouds, water may fall as rain, snow, or hail. What is the term for water, in any form, that falls from the sky?

To answer the question, read each sentence below. If the underlined word is used correctly, write the letter for *correct* in the space above its sentence number. If the underlined word is not used correctly, write the letter for *incorrect*. Some letters are provided.

1. In northern climates, winter snowfalls are <u>ordinary</u> events.
   A. correct   U. incorrect

2. Dad and I went on a <u>vigorous</u> hike yesterday.
   P. correct   M. incorrect

3. People who are <u>impatient</u> are never in a hurry.
   H. correct   I. incorrect

4. The hot sun made the field <u>soggy</u>.
   R. correct   O. incorrect

5. The boring movie was <u>spectacular</u>.
   M. correct   C. incorrect

6. Milk that comes from cows is <u>artificial</u>.
   N. correct   T. incorrect

7. Science is a <u>difficult</u> subject for Paul, but he works hard and does well.
   R. correct   T. incorrect

8. Uncle John has traveled all over the world, and he tells stories of <u>exotic</u> places.
   N. correct   U. incorrect

9. <u>Beautiful</u> means not very pretty.
   S. correct   P. incorrect

10. You should always have a <u>spare</u> tire for your car.
    T. correct   I. incorrect

```
 __   __   E    __   I    __   I    __   __   __   __   __   __
  9    7        5         2         6    1    10   3    4    8
```

Compound Words, I

A compound word is a word that is made of two or more words. Compound words may be closed (for example, *playground*), open (*seat belt*), or hyphenated (*up-to-date*).

1. flashlight (n): a small portable light usually powered by batteries

   We use a <u>flashlight</u> when a storm causes the power to go out during the night.

2. weekend (n): the end of the week, especially Friday evening through Sunday

   Our family relaxes during the <u>weekend</u>.

3. playground (n): an area outside for play and recreation

   Patrick pushed his little brother on the swing at the <u>playground</u>.

4. seat belt (n): a safety belt or strap designed to hold a person securely in a seat

   You should always wear a <u>seat belt</u> when riding in a car.

5. sweatshirt (n): a heavy pullover with long sleeves, often worn during exercise

   Emily wears a <u>sweatshirt</u> when she jogs.

6. tablecloth (n): a cloth or other material used for covering a table, especially during a meal

   Rhiannon put a plastic <u>tablecloth</u> on the picnic table.

7. up-to-date (adj): including the most recent changes; current; modern

Antonio has the most <u>up-to-date</u> software for his computer.

8. sometimes (adv): once in a while; now and then; occasionally

<u>Sometimes</u> Mom lets me stay up late to watch the end of a movie.

9. alarm clock (n): a clock that can be set to ring or buzz at a certain time

I set my <u>alarm clock</u> for seven o'clock each morning.

10. cardboard (n): stiff, heavy paper used in making boxes, signs, posters, etc.

We recycle glass, newspaper, and <u>cardboard</u> every week.

Vocabulary Tip

The meaning of a compound word is usually built upon the meanings of the words that form it.

24.1 Dinosaur Time

Dinosaurs lived throughout the Mesozoic Era. This period of the earth's history lasted from 245 million years ago to 65 million years ago. The Mesozoic Era is often referred to by another name. What is this name?

To answer the question, find the word that matches each definition below. Choose your answers from the words after the definitions. Write the letter of each answer in the space above its definition number at the bottom of the page. You will need to divide the letters into words. Some letters are provided.

1. an area outside for play and recreation _____

2. once in a while; now and then; occasionally _____

3. a small portable light, usually powered by batteries _____

4. including the most recent changes; current; modern _____

5. a heavy pullover with long sleeves _____

6. a clock that can be set to ring or buzz at a certain time _____

7. the end of the week; especially Friday evening through Sunday _____

8. a cloth or other material used for covering a table, especially during a meal _____

9. a safety belt or strap designed to hold a person securely in a seat _____

10. stiff, heavy paper used in making boxes, signs, posters, etc. _____

Answers

A. flashlight
I. up-to-date
O. sweatshirt
E. cardboard
H. sometimes

G. weekend
T. tablecloth
P. playground
L. alarm clock
S. seat belt

<pre>
__ __ __ __ __ __ __   F   R   __ __ __ __ __ __ __
 8   2 10   3   7 10   5   10   1   8   4   6 10   9
</pre>

Compound Words, I

24.2 The Nation's Capital

Washington, DC, is the capital of the United States. What does DC stand for? To answer the question, match each word on the left with the key words of its definition on the right. Write the letter of each answer in the space above the word's number at the bottom of the page. Some letters are provided.

Words

1. playground _____
2. sometimes _____
3. alarm clock _____
4. flashlight _____
5. sweatshirt _____
6. weekend _____
7. up-to-date _____
8. seat belt _____
9. cardboard _____
10. tablecloth _____

Key Words of Definitions

F. portable source of light

C. safety strap when sitting

B. Friday evening through Sunday

I. material used to cover a table

L. current; modern

S. outside area for recreation

T. stiff, heavy paper

M. rings or buzzes at a certain "set" time

D. long-sleeved pullover

O. now and then

__ __ __ R __ __ __   __ __   __ __ __ U __ __ __ A
5 10 1 9   10 8 9   2 4   8 2 7   3 6 10

Compound Words, I

24.3 A President's False Teeth

George Washington had false teeth. What was Washington's first set of false teeth made of?

To answer the question, complete each sentence with the correct word. Choose your answers from the words after the sentences. Write the letter of each answer in the space above its sentence number at the bottom of the page. Some letters are provided.

1. Keeping an _____ assignment pad helps Keisha turn in her work on time.

2. Students at our school spend recess on the _____.

3. When he plays outside on cool days, Jeremy wears a _____.

4. Alison used a _____ to look under the bed for her dog's lost toy.

5. Our new computer was delivered in a box made of thick _____.

6. Mom and I covered the table with a new _____ for dinner.

7. _____ we fish in the stream behind my house.

8. After a hard week of work, Cory looked forward to the _____.

9. I was late for school because I forgot to set my _____.

10. My mom reminds me to wear a _____ in the car.

Answers

U. playground		Y. sometimes
T. weekend		M. flashlight
S. tablecloth		I. sweatshirt
P. seat belt		H. alarm clock
R. up-to-date		O. cardboard

_	I	_	_	_	_	_	A	_	_	_	_	V	_	_	_
9	10	10	5	10	5	8		4	2	6	3		5	1	7

Compound Words, I

Compound Words, II

A compound word is a word that is made of two or more words. Compound words may be closed (for example, *homework*), open (*peanut butter*), or hyphenated (*full-time*).

1. homework (n): work for school that is done at home

   Carla does her <u>homework</u> right after dinner.

2. nearby (adj): a short distance away; close by; (adv): not far away

   My grandparents live in a <u>nearby</u> town.

   My grandparents live <u>nearby</u>.

3. peanut butter (n): a spreadable food made from roasted, ground peanuts

   <u>Peanut butter</u> is one of Joe's favorite snacks.

4. full-time (adj): requiring all of a person's time; working what is considered to be a whole day

   Watching my little sister is a <u>full-time</u> job.

5. newspaper (n): a daily or weekly publication that contains news, advertisements, comics, etc.

   My father reads the <u>newspaper</u> every morning.

6. waterproof (adj): unaffected by water

   I wear <u>waterproof</u> shoes on rainy days.

7. mailbox (n): a box to which mail is delivered or from which it is picked up

   Alex checks the <u>mailbox</u> each day when he comes home from school.

8. somewhere (adv): in or to a place

   I left my glasses <u>somewhere</u> in the house.

9. driveway (n): a road connecting a building to a street

   Dad parks his car in the <u>driveway</u>.

10. fireplace (n): a place for holding a fire

    In the past, a <u>fireplace</u> was the only source of heat for a house.

Vocabulary Tip

Language changes over time. Some open and hyphenated compound words may one day become closed compounds.

25.1 The American Flag

The flag of the United States has some nicknames. One is "Old Glory."
Another is "the Red, White, and Blue." What is a third?

To answer the question, find the word that matches each definition below.
Choose your answers from the words after the definitions. Write the letter of
each answer in the space above its definition number at the bottom of the
page. You will need to divide the letters into words.

1. a box to which mail is delivered or from which it is picked up _____

2. a short distance away _____

3. a daily or weekly publication containing news, advertisements, comics,
   etc. _____

4. a spreadable food made from roasted, ground peanuts _____

5. a road connecting a building to a street _____

6. requiring all of a person's time _____

7. in or to a place _____

8. work for school that is done at home _____

9. a place for holding a fire _____

10. unaffected by water _____

Answers

S. waterproof	D. mailbox
T. driveway	R. somewhere
N. homework	E. fireplace
P. full-time	A. newspaper
I. nearby	H. peanut butter

___ ___ ___ ___ ___ ___ ___ ___ ___ ___ ___ ___ ___ ___ ___ ___ ___ ___
5   4   9 10 5   3   7 10 3   8   1 10 5   7   2   6   9 10

25.2 A State Name

Many American place names come from Native American words. For example, Kentucky comes from the Iroquoian word *kentahten*. What does *kentahten* mean?

To answer the question, match each word on the left with the key words of its definition on the right. Write the letter of each answer in the space above the word's number at the bottom of the page. You will need to divide the letters into words.

Words

1. somewhere _____
2. full-time _____
3. waterproof _____
4. newspaper _____
5. fireplace _____
6. homework _____
7. mailbox _____
8. driveway _____
9. peanut butter _____
10. nearby _____

Key Words of Definitions

W. publication containing news

D. schoolwork done at home

L. road connecting a building to a street

M. requiring all of a person's time

R. box for mail

O. spreadable food made from peanuts

N. unaffected by water

A. not far away

F. holds a fire

T. in or to a place

___ ___ ___ ___ ___ ___ ___ ___ ___ ___ ___ ___ ___ ___
 8   10   3   6   9   5   1   9   2   9   7   7   9   4

25.3 Reading of the Declaration of Independence

The first public reading of the Declaration of Independence was held on July 8, 1776, in Philadelphia. How were citizens called to hear this first reading?

To answer the question, complete each sentence with the correct word. Choose your answers from the words after the sentences. Write the letter of each answer in the space above its sentence number at the bottom of the page. You will need to divide the letters into words. Some letters are provided.

1. Every summer we walk to a _____ lake and go swimming.

2. Erica's _____ coat keeps her dry in rainy weather.

3. Tim knew his keys had to be _____ in the house.

4. Dave checked the _____ for a birthday card from his grandmother.

5. Hannah's mom works _____ at the post office.

6. Mrs. Parker reads the _____ on the train on her way to work.

7. Our teacher does not assign _____ on the weekends.

8. The _____ from the road to the mountain cabin was long and windy.

9. Wood burning in the _____ provided heat to the room.

10. Many people like to spread _____ on bananas and apples.

Answers

T. newspaper	E. mailbox
N. waterproof	R. driveway
B. fireplace	O. somewhere
I. full-time	Y. nearby
L. peanut butter	G. homework

```
 __   __   __   __   __   __   __   __   F    __   H    __
 8    5    2    7    5    2    7    3         6         4

 __   __   __   __   __   __   __   __   __   __   __
 10   5    9    4    8    6    1    9    4    10   10
```

Words Based on Names

An eponym is a word that comes from the name of a person. A toponym is a word that comes from the name of a place. Some words are based on the names of gods and goddesses of mythology.

1. cereal (n): a food made from grain, such as wheat, oats, or corn often eaten for breakfast

   The word <u>cereal</u> comes from Ceres, the Roman goddess of agriculture.

2. Braille (n): a system of writing with raised dots used by blind people for reading

   Louis Braille, a blind French teacher, invented <u>Braille</u>.

3. saxophone (n): a musical instrument

   Antoine Sax, a Belgian instrument maker, invented the <u>saxophone</u>.

4. frankfurter (n): a sausage made of beef or beef and pork, commonly called a hot dog

   The <u>frankfurter</u> is named after the German city of Frankfurt.

5. limerick (n): a humorous poem of five lines with the rhyme pattern AABBA

   The <u>limerick</u> is named for the county of Limerick in Ireland.

6. sandwich (n): slices of bread with meat, cheese, or another food between them

   The <u>sandwich</u> is named after Englishman John Montagu, the Earl of Sandwich.

7. volcano (n): a mountain formed by lava that rises through openings in the earth's surface

   The word <u>volcano</u> comes from Vulcan, the Roman god of fire.

8. Ferris wheel (n): a big upright, turning wheel with hanging seats; a ride at amusement parks

   George Ferris invented the <u>Ferris wheel</u> in 1893.

9. Fahrenheit (adj): pertaining to a temperature scale with the freezing point of water at 32 degrees and the boiling point at 212 degrees

   Gabriel Fahrenheit, a German scientist, invented the <u>Fahrenheit</u> thermometer.

10. Celsius (adj): pertaining to a temperature scale with the freezing point of water at 0 degrees and the boiling point at 100 degrees

    Anders Celsius, a Swedish scientist, invented the <u>Celsius</u> thermometer.

Vocabulary Tip

Eponyms, toponyms, and words based on mythology have interesting origins.

26.1 Planets of Our Solar System

The eight planets of our solar system are Mercury, Venus, Earth, Mars, Jupiter, Saturn, Uranus, and Neptune. Four of the planets are made mostly of gas and are not solid. The other four are solid, rocky bodies. Which planets in our solar system are rocky bodies?

To answer the question, find the word that matches each definition below. Choose your answers from the words after the definitions. Write the letter of each answer in the space above its definition number at the bottom of the page. You will need to divide the letters into words. Some letters are provided.

1. pertaining to a temperature scale that shows water freezing at 32 degrees and boiling at 212 degrees _____

2. a humorous poem of five lines with the rhyme pattern AABBA _____

3. two or more slices of bread with meat, cheese, or another food between them _____

4. a system of writing with raised dots used by blind people for reading _____

5. a big upright, turning wheel with hanging seats _____

6. a mountain formed by lava that rises through openings in the earth's surface _____

7. a food made from grain such as wheat, oats, or corn _____

8. a musical instrument _____

9. pertaining to a temperature scale that shows water freezing at 0 degrees and boiling at 100 degrees _____

10. a sausage commonly called a hot dog _____

© Gary Robert Muschla

Answers

U. cereal

R. frankfurter

E. limerick

H. saxophone

N. Fahrenheit

Y. volcano

A. Braille

M. Celsius

V. Ferris wheel

S. sandwich

<u> </u> <u> </u> <u> </u> <u>T</u> <u> </u> <u> </u> <u> </u> <u> </u> <u>C</u> <u> </u> <u> </u> <u> </u>

 2   4   10   8   9   2   10   7   10   6

<u> </u> <u> </u> <u> </u> <u> </u> <u> </u> <u> </u> <u> </u> <u> </u>

 9   4   10   3   5   2   1   7   3

26.2 First Balloon Flight in America

In 1793, this Frenchman made the first balloon flight in America. He took off in Philadelphia and landed in Gloucester County, New Jersey. Who was he?

To answer the question, complete each sentence with the correct word. Choose your answers from the words after the sentences. Write the letter of each answer in the space above its sentence number at the bottom of the page. Some letters are provided.

1. We like to ride the _____ at the amusement park.

2. Jillian's mom packs her a ham _____ for lunch.

3. Lila eats _____ for breakfast every morning.

4. For his assignment to write a poem, Josh wrote a _____.

5. My grandfather calls a hot dog a _____.

6. An erupting _____ can cause much destruction.

7. On a _____ thermometer, water freezes at 32 degrees.

8. Jimmy plays the _____ in the school band.

9. After learning _____, blind people are able to read.

10. On a _____ thermometer, water boils at 100 degrees.

Answers

E. Celsius   P. limerick
R. Braille   B. saxophone
A. cereal   J. frankfurter
H. volcano   N. Fahrenheit
D. Ferris wheel   C. sandwich

```
__   __   __   __        __   I    __   __   __   __
 5   10    3    7         4        10    9    9   10

__   L    __   __   __   __   __   __
 8         3    7    2    6    3    9    1
```

Words Based on Names

26.3 A Renewable Form of Energy

This renewable form of energy uses heat that rises from deep within the earth. What is the name of this form of energy?

To answer the question, read each sentence below. If the underlined word is used correctly, write the letter for *correct* in the space above its sentence number at the bottom of the page. If the underlined word is not used correctly, write the letter for *incorrect*.

1. A frankfurter is a sausage made of beef or beef and pork.
   E. correct   O. incorrect

2. A volcano is a valley between two mountains.
   C. correct   T. incorrect

3. A limerick is a poem about Ireland.
   I. correct   A. incorrect

4. My Aunt Tina is blind, but she can read with Braille.
   R. correct   M. incorrect

5. A Ferris wheel is usually found at an amusement park or carnival.
   O. correct   U. incorrect

6. The boiling point of water on a Celsius thermometer is 212 degrees.
   R. correct   L. incorrect

7. Tommy practices his saxophone every evening.
   H. correct   O. incorrect

8. Mika put ham between two slices of bread to make a sandwich.
   G. correct   M. incorrect

9. The freezing point of water on a Fahrenheit thermometer is 0 degrees.
   Y. correct   E. incorrect

10. Cereal is a type of meat used in making sandwiches.
    T. correct   M. incorrect

— — — — — — — — — —
8   9   5   2   7   1   4   10   3   6

Portmanteau Words

Portmanteau words are words that blend the sounds and combine the meanings of two words. Portmanteau words are also known as "blends."

1. brash (adj): hasty; rash; unthinking (from *bold* and *rash*)

   Derrick is a <u>brash</u> young man.

2. splurge (v): to spend excessively (from *splash* and *surge*)

   My older sister likes to <u>splurge</u> at the mall.

3. brunch (n): a meal that is a combination of breakfast and lunch (from *breakfast* and *lunch*)

   We went to <u>brunch</u> on Sunday.

4. flop (v): to fall down heavily (from *flap* and *drop*)

   Tonya was tired and wanted to <u>flop</u> on the couch.

5. motel (n): a hotel for people traveling by car (from *motor* and *hotel*)

   We stayed overnight in a <u>motel</u> on our drive to visit my grandparents.

6. smog (n): fog that is mixed with smoke and pollution (from *smoke* and *fog*)

   The <u>smog</u> was very thick in the city.

7. smash (v): to break violently; to shatter (from *smack* and *mash*)

   The big wave will <u>smash</u> the sand castle.

8. moped (n): a motorized bicycle (from *motor* and *pedal*)

   Michael rides his <u>moped</u> on his grandfather's farm.

9. chortle (n): a snorting, happy chuckle; (v): to utter a snorting, happy chuckle (from *chuckle* and *snort*)

   Morgan's baby brother will <u>chortle</u> when he's happy.

   The clown began his act with a <u>chortle</u>.

10. squiggle (n): a wiggly mark; a scrawl; (v): to squirm and wriggle (from *squirm* and *wriggle*)

    While doodling, Rosa made a <u>squiggle</u> on her paper.

    My baby brother likes to <u>squiggle</u> around the floor.

Vocabulary Tip

Portmanteau is a French word that means "suitcase." Just as two parts of a suitcase close into one piece of luggage, portmanteau words have two parts that become one word. Their meanings usually are based on the meanings of the words that they are formed from.

Portmanteau Words

27.1 Breathing

When we exercise, we breathe faster than when we are resting. About how many times per minute does the average adult breathe when resting?

To answer the question, find the word that matches each definition below. Choose your answers from the words that follow each definition. Write the letter of each answer in the space above its definition number at the bottom of the page. You will need to divide the letters into words. Some letters are provided.

1. a wiggly mark; a scrawl
   A. chortle   I. brash   E. squiggle

2. a meal that is a combination of breakfast and lunch
   T. brunch   N. smog   U. splurge

3. a hotel for people traveling by car
   E. squiggle   W. flop   T. motel

4. to break violently; to shatter
   F. chortle   T. smash   S. squiggle

5. fog mixed with smoke and pollution
   T. smog   U. smash   N. chortle

6. a snorting, happy chuckle
   O. flop   W. chortle   H. smash

7. to spend excessively
   E. moped   T. brunch   N. splurge

8. to fall down heavily
   L. flop   R. smash   E. brash

9. a motorized bicycle
   U. smash   R. chortle   W. moped

10. hasty; rash; unthinking
    T. moped   V. brash   Y. squiggle

__ __ E __ __ __ __ O __ __ E __ __ Y
4 6   8 10 1 2   5 9   7 3

27.2 Inventor of the Dishwasher

This woman invented the dishwasher in 1886. Who was she?

To answer the question, match each word on the left with the words that it is formed from on the right. Write the letter of each answer in the space above the word's number at the bottom of the page. Some letters are provided.

Words	Forming Words
1. smog _____	P. bold and rash
2. moped _____	H. smack and mash
3. brunch _____	S. motor and pedal
4. brash _____	J. chuckle and snort
5. motel _____	O. flap and drop
6. smash _____	N. splash and surge
7. flop _____	R. breakfast and lunch
8. chortle _____	E. squirm and wriggle
9. squiggle _____	A. smoke and fog
10. splurge _____	C. motor and hotel

_ _ _ E _ _ I _ _   _ _ _ _ _ _ _
8 7 2   4 6   10 9   5 7 5 6 3 1 10

27.3 A Prairie Author

This author was 65 years old when she published her first book. She wrote about life on the prairie. Who was she?

To answer the question, complete each sentence with the correct word. Choose your answers from the words after the sentences. Write the letter of each answer in the space above its sentence number at the bottom of the page. One letter is provided.

1. Kevin's favorite pastime is riding his _____.

2. After waking up late, Mom and I went to a diner for _____.

3. The _____ was so thick that we could barely see.

4. Our dog tried to _____ under the fence.

5. When we go shopping, we try not to _____.

6. The teacher asked who was making a _____ and disturbing the class.

7. After driving all day, we spent the night in a _____.

8. Manuel is always in a hurry and can be very _____.

9. Our dog likes to _____ on her pillow after playing outside.

10. The karate expert tried to _____ a board with his bare hand.

Answers

E. chortle	U. splurge	N. moped	R. smog	L. smash
D. brunch	W. brash	I. squiggle	G. flop	A. motel

__ __ __ __ __ __ __ __ __ __ __ S __ __ __ __ __ __
10 7 5 3 7   4 1 9 7 10 10   8 4 10 2 6 3

Clipped Words

Many long words are shortened by common use. These words are referred to as clipped words.

1. burger (n): a hamburger; a sandwich made with a patty of ground meat, usually beef

   Martin ate a <u>burger</u> for dinner.

2. ump (n): umpire; a person who rules on the plays of a game

   The <u>ump</u> called Ellie out at first base.

3. gym (n): gymnasium; a room for exercise or sports

   We played basketball in the <u>gym</u>.

4. math (n): mathematics; the science that deals with numbers and measurement

   <u>Math</u> is Katie's favorite subject because she is good with numbers.

5. champ (n): champion; a person who holds first place or wins first prize in a contest or sports event

   Nicholas is the <u>champ</u> of the fifth-grade 100-yard dash.

6. flu (n): influenza; an illness with fever, sore throat, body aches, and fatigue caused by a virus

   Colin had the <u>flu</u> and missed a week of school.

7. plane (n): airplane; a winged vehicle capable of flying

   Our family traveled to Chicago by <u>plane</u>.

8. condo (n): condominium; an apartment that is owned rather than rented

   Ben's grandparents live in a <u>condo</u> in Florida.

9. fridge (n): refrigerator; a box, cabinet, or room for storing foods or other substances at low temperatures

   Ann helped her mother put the groceries into the <u>fridge</u>.

10. deli (n): delicatessen; a shop that sells foods ready for serving

    Dad bought sandwiches at the <u>deli</u> for lunch.

Vocabulary Tip

Clipped words have the same meaning as their longer forms.

28.1 Life in the Sea

One type of scientist studies plants and animals that live in the ocean. What is this scientist called?

To answer the question, match each clipped word on the left with its longer form on the right. Write the letter of each answer in the space above the clipped word's number at the bottom of the page. Some letters are provided.

Clipped Words	**Longer Forms**
1. condo _____	L. champion
2. burger _____	T. umpire
3. gym _____	I. refrigerator
4. champ _____	B. mathematics
5. plane _____	R. influenza
6. ump _____	A. gymnasium
7. flu _____	O. delicatessen
8. deli _____	E. condominium
9. math _____	M. airplane
10. fridge _____	G. hamburger

___ ___ ___ ___ N̲ ___   ___ ___ ___ ___ ___ ___ ___ S̲ ___
 5   3   7 10   1   9 10   8   4   8   2 10   6

28.2 Named for a Queen

The colony of Maryland was named after the queen of Charles I of England. What was the queen's name?

To answer the question, find the word for each definition below. Choose your answers from the words that follow each definition. Write the letter of each answer in the space above its definition number at the bottom of the page. Some letters are provided.

1. a winged vehicle capable of flying

    R. condo   I. deli   N. plane

2. a box, cabinet, or room for storing foods or other substances at low temperatures

    S. champ   N. gym   A. fridge

3. a sandwich made with a patty of ground meat, usually beef

    T. burger   I. flu   O. condo

4. a shop that sells foods ready for serving

    U. gym   R. deli   A. burger

5. a person who rules on the plays of a game

    I. ump   Y. champ   S. fridge

6. an apartment that is owned rather than rented

    A. plane   N. deli   E. condo

7. the science that deals with numbers and measurement

    D. gym   M. math   A. champ

8. an illness with fever, sore throat, body aches, and fatigue caused by a virus

    U. condo   E. flu   O. ump

9. a person who holds first place or wins first place in a contest or sports event

    H. champ   M. ump   A. gym

10. a room for exercise or sports

    N. plane   R. gym   S. condo

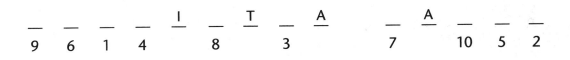

$\underline{}$ $\underline{}$ $\underline{}$ $\underline{}$ $\underline{I}$ $\underline{}$ $\underline{T}$ $\underline{}$ $\underline{A}$ $\underline{}$ $\underline{A}$ $\underline{}$ $\underline{}$ $\underline{}$

9   6   1   4   8   3   7   10   5   2

28.3 Parts of the Earth

The equator divides the earth into two equal parts. What are these parts, or halves, called?

To answer the question, complete each sentence with the correct word. Choose your answers from the words after each sentence. Write the letter of each answer in the space above its sentence number at the bottom of the page. One letter is provided.

1. We visited my Aunt Emily at her _____ in New York.
   E. condo   U. plane   I. fridge

2. It is poor sportsmanship to argue with the _____.
   R. champ   N. gym   S. ump

3. Shane likes working with numbers and does well in _____.
   U. deli   E. math   I. gym

4. Stephanie was the _____ of the fourth-grade spelling bee.
   A. plane   U. condo   E. champ

5. After dinner, Dad put the leftovers in the _____.
   U. condo   I. fridge   A. deli

6. Scott was sick with the _____ last week.
   N. math   T. gym   R. flu

7. Dad grilled a _____ for me and hot dogs for everyone else.
   P. burger   M. deli   C. fridge

8. We always buy our meat from the _____.
   R. burger   H. deli   O. condo

9. The fastest way to get from New York to Los Angeles is by _____.
   H. plane   S. condo   M. flu

10. We played floor hockey in the _____.
    N. condo   C. deli   M. gym

__	__	__	__	S	__	__	__	__	__	__
9	4	10	5		7	8	1	6	3	2

Words from Other Languages, I

English contains many words that come from other languages.

1. rodeo (n): a competition or show featuring skills such as horseback riding, bull riding, and lassoing (from Spanish)

   The most exciting event at the <u>rodeo</u> was the bull riding.

2. yacht (n): a relatively small ship used for pleasure (from Dutch)

   Melissa enjoyed sailing on her uncle's <u>yacht</u>.

3. mustang (n): a wild horse (from Spanish)

   The <u>mustang</u> galloped across the prairie.

4. haiku (n): a poem of 17 syllables (from Japanese)

   Terence wrote a <u>haiku</u> for his school's poetry magazine.

5. patio (n): an outdoor space that is near a home and is used for eating and relaxing (from Spanish)

   We ate dinner on our <u>patio</u> last night.

6. macaroni (n): a type of noodle in the shape of hollow tubes, prepared for eating by boiling (from Italian)

   Gena's favorite food is <u>macaroni</u> with cheese.

7. depot (n): a bus or railroad station; a storehouse (from French)

   People waited at the <u>depot</u> for the train to come.

8. waffle (n): a batter cake cooked between two metal plates (from Dutch)

   Mom cooked a <u>waffle</u> for me for breakfast.

9. umbrella (n): a device made of a light frame and cover for protection against rain and sun (from Italian)

   Stacy's <u>umbrella</u> protected her from the rain.

10. chef (n): a cook; the chief cook in a restaurant (from French)

    Matt likes to cook and hopes to be a <u>chef</u> someday.

Vocabulary Tip

English is constantly growing as people add new words from other languages.

29.1 A Colonial Tune

British soldiers sang this song to make fun of American colonists. In time the colonists adopted the song as their own. What was the title of this song?

To answer the question, find the word for each definition below. Choose your answers from the words that follow each definition. Write the letter of each answer in the space above its definition number at the bottom of the page. You will need to divide the letters into words. Some letters are provided.

1. an outdoor space that is near a home and used for eating and relaxing
   H. depot   A. patio   E. rodeo

2. a batter cake cooked between two metal plates
   E. waffle   N. haiku   C. yacht

3. a cook; the chief cook of a restaurant
   A. macaroni   E. mustang   N. chef

4. a wild horse
   D. mustang   E. patio   R. waffle

5. a competition or show featuring skills such as horseback riding, bull riding, and lassoing
   D. haiku   L. rodeo   N. mustang

6. a type of noodle in the shape of hollow tubes, prepared for eating by boiling
   G. waffle   N. chef   E. macaroni

7. a Japanese poem of 17 syllables
   B. depot   M. yacht   D. haiku

8. a device made of a light frame and cover for protection against rain and sun
   N. patio   K. umbrella   R. waffle

9. a relatively small ship used for pleasure
   Y. yacht   S. mustang   W. depot

10. a bus or railroad station; a storehouse
    U. patio   A. yacht   O. depot

___	___	___	___	E	___	___	O	___	___	___	___
9	1	3	8	6	7		10	4	5	2	

Words from Other Languages, I

29.2 A Special Means of Communication

Many deaf people use a system of gestures, facial expressions, and a hand alphabet to communicate. What is this system called?

To answer the question, read each sentence below. Replace each under-lined word or phrase with the word or phrase that has a similar meaning. Choose your answers from the words after each sentence. Write the letter of each answer in the space above its sentence number at the bottom of the page. You will need to divide the letters into words. Some letters are provided.

1. The <u>wild horse</u> was one of the most beautiful horses Liza had ever seen.
   D. waffle   S. haiku   E. mustang

2. We had a great time at the <u>show that had horseback riding, bull riding, and rope tricks.</u>
   L. depot   G. rodeo   N. patio

3. To protect ourselves from the sun when we are at the beach, we sit under <u>a device with a dark cover.</u>
   A. a waffle   I. an umbrella   H. a yacht

4. We ate salad and <u>noodles</u> with cheese for dinner last night.
   G. macaroni   I. waffle   D. patio

5. Lenny arrived at the <u>station</u> just in time for the bus.
   N. depot   T. patio   O. haiku

6. We enjoyed an evening cruise on the <u>ship.</u>
   E. chef   A. yacht   U. rodeo

7. Gloria cooked a thick <u>batter cake between two metal plates.</u>
   I. macaroni   S. haiku   U. waffle

8. Dad set up the hammock on the <u>space outside next to our house.</u>
   A. umbrella   S. patio   P. depot

9. We had to write a <u>Japanese poem of 17 syllables</u> for homework.
   G. haiku   C. rodeo   R. mustang

10. Mom complimented the <u>cook</u> for our excellent dinners at the restaurant.
   U. macaroni   M. waffle   L. chef

__	__	__	__	__	__	N	__	__	A	__
8	3	9	5	10	6	2	7		4	1

29.3 Salesman for a Silly Toy

A stretchy material that came to be called Silly Putty was developed at General Electric in 1944. In 1949, a man began selling Silly Putty in plastic eggs. Who was the man who first sold Silly Putty?

To answer the question, complete each sentence with the correct word. Choose your answers from the words after the sentences. Write the letter of each answer in the space above its sentence number at the bottom of the page.

1. The restaurant's _____ prepared delicious meals.

2. The _____ is a Japanese poem of 17 syllables.

3. I helped Mom boil _____ for dinner.

4. Lisa's father works at a bus _____.

5. Cowboys and cowgirls rode horses and performed rope tricks in the town's annual _____.

6. I forgot my _____ and got soaked in the rain.

7. I enjoy relaxing on the _____ when the weather is warm.

8. Sean's uncle Danny sails to Florida on his _____ every summer.

9. The _____ was cooked perfectly on both sides.

10. The powerful _____ was the leader of a herd of wild horses.

Answers

S. haiku   E. rodeo
R. patio   O. mustang
P. waffle   D. chef
H. depot   G. umbrella
N. macaroni   T. yacht

___ ___ ___ ___ ___   ___ ___ ___ ___ ___ ___ ___
 9   5   8   5   7   4 10   1   6   2 10   3

Words from Other Languages, II

English contains many words that come from other languages.

1. hurricane (n): a very powerful storm that begins over the ocean (from Spanish)

   People left the island before the <u>hurricane</u> struck.

2. ballet (n): a formal dance with graceful movements (from French)

   <u>Ballet</u> is Samantha's favorite dance.

3. knapsack (n): a bag made of canvas or leather that is carried on the back (from German)

   Jake packed his <u>knapsack</u> for a long hike.

4. mayor (n): the head of a town or city government (from French)

   The <u>mayor</u> called an emergency meeting of the town's council.

5. judge (n): a person who presides over a court of law and makes legal rulings (from French)

   Everyone rose when the <u>judge</u> entered the courtroom.

6. pasta (n): a food such as spaghetti or macaroni

   Jamie had <u>pasta</u> for dinner.

7. tornado (n): a violent storm with whirling winds in the shape of a funnel cloud (from Spanish)

   The <u>tornado</u> left a path of destruction.

8. justice (n): fairness (from French)

   The laws must provide <u>justice</u> for everyone.

9. canyon (n): a gorge with steep sides; a ravine (from Spanish)

   The explorers set up their camp on high ground above the <u>canyon</u>.

10. bandit (n): an outlaw; a robber; a thief (from Italian)

   According to legend, Robin Hood was a <u>bandit</u> who helped the poor.

Vocabulary Tip

Many people around the world speak English.

Words from Other Languages, II

30.1 Making Driving Safer

In 1923, Garrett A. Morgan invented a device that made driving by automobile safer. What did Morgan invent?

To answer the question, find the word for each definition below. Choose your answers from the words after the definitions. Write the letter of each answer in the space above its definition number at the bottom of the page. You will need to divide the letters into words. Some letters are provided.

1. a gorge with steep sides; a ravine _____

2. a person who presides over a court of law and makes legal rulings _____

3. a food such as spaghetti or macaroni _____

4. a very powerful storm that begins over the ocean _____

5. a bag made of canvas or leather that is carried on the back _____

6. the head of a town or city government _____

7. an outlaw; a robber; a thief _____

8. fairness _____

9. a formal dance with graceful movements _____

10. a violent storm with whirling winds in the shape of a funnel cloud _____

Answers

N. bandit   S. pasta
C. canyon   I. mayor
T. justice   L. knapsack
M. judge   O. hurricane
A. ballet   F. tornado

```
___  U   ___  ___  ___  ___  ___  ___  ___     R   ___  ___  ___  ___  ___
 9       8    4    2    9    8    6    1    8        9   10   10    6    1

          ___  ___   G   ___  ___  ___
           3    6         7    9    5
```

30.2 A Folk Hero

In American folklore, this man was said to be the greatest sailor of all. Who was he?

To answer the question, complete each sentence with the correct word. Choose your answers from the words after the sentences. Write the letter of each answer in the space above its sentence number at the bottom of the page. You will need to divide the letters into words.

1. The people demanded _____ from the wicked king.

2. The _____ called the town's public meeting to order.

3. The police caught the _____ with the stolen money.

4. The steep sides of the _____ protected the village from harsh winds.

5. The _____ ordered the people in the courtroom to be silent.

6. One of Rosie's favorite foods is _____.

7. It takes years of dance practice to learn the graceful movements of _____.

8. With its whirling winds in the shape of a funnel cloud, the _____ is a frightening storm.

9. Ty's _____ was so heavy that he could barely lift the bag onto his back.

10. A _____ is a great storm that forms over the ocean.

Answers

S. judge   N. mayor
T. bandit   D. hurricane
L. pasta   O. tornado
A. ballet   R. canyon
G. knapsack   M. justice

—   —   —   —   —   —   —   —   —   —   —   —   —
8   6   10   5   3   8   4   1   7   6   8   2   9

Words from Other Languages, II

30.3 Delaware's Name

Delaware was one of the original 13 colonies. Its name comes from the formal title of Englishman Sir Thomas West. What was Sir Thomas West's title?

To answer the question, read each sentence below. Replace the underlined word or phrase with the word or phrase that has a similar meaning. Choose your answers from the words after each sentence. Write the letter of each answer in the space above its sentence number at the bottom of the page. Some letters are provided.

1. A bandit broke into the bank last night.
   E. judge   O. mayor   A. thief

2. We went to an Italian restaurant for a spaghetti dinner.
   A. a knapsack   R. pasta   E. a canyon

3. The person in charge of the courtroom listened to the evidence before giving his ruling.
   S. mayor   N. judge   R. bandit

4. Patrick's father is the head of his town's government.
   O. mayor   E. judge   U. canyon

5. We went to the city to watch a formal dance with graceful movements.
   V. pasta   L. hurricane   D. ballet

6. Ryan slipped his arms into the straps of the heavy canvas bag.
   W. knapsack   S. canyon   D. ballet

7. Our laws guarantee fairness for our citizens.
   M. judge   B. justice   R. mayor

8. The view overlooking the ravine was wonderful.
   A. canyon   E. tornado   I. ballet

9. Weather forecasters warned that the powerful ocean storm was headed for the coast.
   I. tornado   U. pasta   A. hurricane

10. The funnel cloud with its violent winds just missed the town.
    V. hurricane   L. tornado   S. bandit

__	__	R	__	__	__	E	__	__	__	__	__	R
7	9	4	3		5		10	1	6	8	2	

Contractions

A contraction is a short form of two words. An apostrophe is used to show where a letter or letters have been left out.

1. I'm: I am

   I'm finished with my homework.

2. it's: it is

   It's going to rain today.

3. you've: you have

   You've been chosen to be the team's captain.

4. we'll: we will

   We'll meet you at the restaurant.

5. we're: we are

   We're looking forward to the start of the baseball season.

6. they're: they are

   They're in the library studying.

7. won't: will not

   I won't be able to go to Tina's party.

8. you're: you are

   You're the student of the month.

9. doesn't: does not

   If Franco <u>doesn't</u> hurry, he will be late.

10. he's: he is

    <u>He's</u> the fastest runner in the fifth grade.

Vocabulary Tip

Be careful not to confuse the following words:
- *you're* (you are) with the possessive pronoun *your*
- *they're* (they are) with the possessive pronoun *their* and the adverb *there*
- *it's* (it is) with the possessive pronoun *its*
- *we're* (we are) with the verb *were*

31.1 A New State

This area broke away from a state that left the Union at the beginning of the Civil War. The area became a new state during the war. What state is this?

To answer the question, match the words on the left with the contraction they form on the right. Write the letter of each answer in the space above the word's number at the bottom of the page. You will need to divide the letters into words.

Words

1. will not _____

2. he is _____

3. I am _____

4. we are _____

5. it is _____

6. they are _____

7. you are _____

8. you have _____

9. does not _____

10. we will _____

Contractions

N. he's

T. it's

S. you're

A. we're

I. doesn't

R. won't

V. we'll

G. they're

W. you've

E. I'm

__ __ __ __ __ __ __ __ __ __ __ __
8   3   7   5   10   9   1   6   9   2   9   4

31.2 Making a Good Thing Better

In 1881, Lewis Latimer made one of Thomas Edison's greatest inventions even better. What did Latimer make?

To answer the question, read each sentence below. Replace each underlined word or words with the word or words that mean the same. Choose your answers from the words after the sentences. (Not all answers will be used.) Write the letter of each answer in the space above its sentence number at the bottom of the page. You will need to divide the letters into words. Some letters are provided.

1. We <u>won't</u> have school because of the snowstorm. _____

2. <u>You've</u> been assigned the third seat on the bus. _____

3. <u>It is</u> almost time for lunch. _____

4. I hope the rain <u>does not</u> start until after the game is finished. _____

5. <u>We are</u> going shopping at the mall. _____

6. <u>They are</u> leaving for Denver tomorrow. _____

7. <u>I'm</u> the youngest in my family. _____

8. <u>You are</u> the new team captain. _____

9. <u>We'll</u> start our project after school. _____

10. <u>He's</u> the new student in school. _____

Answers

G. you're	S. its	R. will not
B. he is	L. I am	M. we will
Y. were	E. it's	W. their
I. they're	N. your	P. we're
A. there	V. you have	T. doesn't

__ __ __ __ O __ __ D __ __ __ H __ __ U __ __
6 9 5 1   2 3   7 6 8   4 10   7 10

31.3 Colonial Protest

In 1773, colonists dressed up as Native Americans. They then protested a tax they believed was unfair. What event was this?

To answer the question, complete each sentence with the correct word. Choose your answers from the words after each sentence. Write the letter of each answer in the space above its sentence number at the bottom of the page. You will need to divide the letters into words. One letter is provided.

1. _____ the only boy who is a finalist in the geography contest.
   T. You've   S. He's   C. We'll

2. _____ one of two sets of twins in the fourth grade.
   R. They're   M. Their   U. There

3. _____ meet at Tommy's house after school.
   A. You're   I. We're   E. We'll

4. _____ going to a concert with my sister.
   H. Your   A. I'm   N. We'll

5. _____ moving to Virginia next year.
   Y. We're   C. You've   L. Were

6. The puppy _____ have his collar.
   J. he's   W. its   P. doesn't

7. We _____ have to leave until after dinner.
   H. won't   T. doesn't   N. were

8. _____ been chosen to be the leader of the first group.
   U. You're   E. Your   O. You've

9. _____ going to rain all day.
   R. There   L. Its   B. It's

10. _____ the tallest student in class.
    M. They're   T. You're   I. Your

__ __ __ __ __ __ __ N __ __ __ __ __ __ __ __
10 7 3 9 8 1 10 8   10 3 4 6 4 2 10 5

Words for Readers and Writers

Readers and writers use many of the same words.

1. author (n): a writer

   Beverly Cleary is my favorite <u>author</u>.

2. character (n): a person in a story

   The lead <u>character</u> in the story was a fifth-grade student.

3. plot (n): a series of events that move a story forward

   The story had an exciting <u>plot</u> with a lot of action.

4. fiction (n): a story in which the events and characters are mostly imagined

   A novel is an example of <u>fiction</u>.

5. nonfiction (n): writing that is based on facts and not imagination

   A true story is an example of <u>nonfiction</u>.

6. setting (n): the times and places where the events of a story happen

   The <u>setting</u> of Jacob's story was a moon base in the future.

7. opening (n): the beginning of a piece of writing; the beginning of a story

   Su Lin wrote a new <u>opening</u> for her story.

8. closing (n): the end of a piece of writing; the end of a story; the conclusion

   The <u>closing</u> of the story left me feeling sad.

9. detail (n): a trait or part of someone or something

The most memorable <u>detail</u> about the bear was its size.

10. dialogue (n): a conversation between two or more characters

In Ernesto's story, the <u>dialogue</u> of the characters was very interesting.

Vocabulary Tip

Many subjects have a special vocabulary.

Words for Readers and Writers

32.1 A Bolt of Lightning

Lightning is one of nature's most powerful wonders. What is lightning?

To answer the question, find the word for each definition below. Choose your answers from the words that follow each definition. Write the letter of each answer in the space above its definition number at the bottom of the page. Some letters are provided.

1. the beginning of a piece of writing
   C. opening   R. dialogue   N. detail

2. a series of events that move a story forward
   H. setting   R. plot   S. character

3. a story in which the events and characters are mostly imagined
   U. detail   A. fiction   E. nonfiction

4. a conversation between two or more characters
   O. setting   Y. detail   E. dialogue

5. the end of a piece of writing; the end of a story
   T. closing   K. plot   S. opening

6. a trait or part of someone or something
   D. setting   T. detail   M. fiction

7. a person in a story
   R. detail   H. dialogue   C. character

8. the times and places where the events of a story happen
   I. opening   T. plot   L. setting

9. writing that is based on facts and not imagination
   S. fiction   Y. nonfiction   N. closing

10. a writer
    S. author   C. dialogue   T. character

```
__  T   __  __  I   __      E   __  __  C   T   __  I   __  I   __  __
10      3   6   1           8   4           2       7       5   9
```

32.2 Primary and Secondary Colors

The primary colors are red, blue, and yellow. What are the secondary colors? To answer the question, complete each sentence with the correct word. Choose your answers from the words after the sentences. Write the letter of each answer in the space above its sentence number at the bottom of the page. You will need to divide the letters into words.

1. The _____ of the characters made them sound like real people.

2. The _____ of the story was colonial Virginia.

3. After reading the story's _____, I wanted to read the rest of the book.

4. Superman is Connor's favorite comic book _____.

5. A story about real people and true events is _____.

6. A great _____ can help your imagination "picture" a character or setting.

7. The _____ of the story kept the action moving forward.

8. A story that is based on a writer's imagination is _____.

9. A. A. Milne is the _____ of *Winnie the Pooh*.

10. The _____ of the story showed the characters finally getting home.

Answers

E. author	L. opening
O. plot	T. dialogue
V. fiction	G. closing
A. setting	I. nonfiction
R. detail	N. character

___ ___ ___ ___ ___ ___ ___ ___ ___ ___ ___ ___ ___ ___ ___ ___ ___
8 5 7 3 9 1 10 6 9 9 4 7 6 2 4 10 9

Words for Readers and Writers

32.3 Memphis

An American president named the city of Memphis, Tennessee. He named it after the ancient city of Memphis in Egypt. Ancient Memphis was a center of government, learning, and religion. Which president named Memphis, Tennessee?

To answer the question, read each sentence below. If the underlined word is used correctly, write the letter for *correct* in the space above its sentence number at the bottom of the page. If the underlined word is not used correctly, write the letter for *incorrect*. You will need to divide the letters into words. One letter is provided.

1. The <u>setting</u> of a story tells about the characters.
   A. correct   E. incorrect

2. A <u>detail</u> can give information about someone.
   C. correct   F. incorrect

3. A written account that tells the true story of an event is <u>fiction</u>.
   E. correct   N. incorrect

4. A <u>dialogue</u> is a conversation between characters.
   S. correct   R. incorrect

5. The <u>plot</u> of a story tells where a story happens.
   M. correct   R. incorrect

6. A story's <u>closing</u> comes at the story's beginning.
   S. correct   W. incorrect

7. A <u>character</u> is a person in a story.
   J. correct   A. incorrect

8. <u>Nonfiction</u> is based on both facts and the author's imagination.
   T. correct   A. incorrect

9. The <u>opening</u> is the point where a story begins.
   K. correct   O. incorrect

10. An <u>author</u> writes a story.
    D. correct   O. incorrect

__ __ __ __ __ __ __ __ __ __ __ O̲ __
8   3   10 5   1   6   7   8   2   9   4   3

Math Words

Mathematics is a subject that has a special vocabulary.

1. **estimate** (n): a guess or opinion about the size, amount, etc. of something; (v): to guess the size, amount, etc. of something

   An <u>estimate</u> is not an exact number.

   We tried to <u>estimate</u> the cost of our vacation.

2. **solution** (n): an answer; an explanation

   Victoria found the <u>solution</u> to the math puzzle.

3. **fraction** (n): a number that names a part of a whole or a part of a group

   A <u>fraction</u> has a numerator and a denominator.

4. **measure** (n): a unit used to find the length, width, weight, etc. of something; (v): to find the length, width, weight, etc. of something

   An inch is a unit of <u>measure</u> for length.

   For homework, we must <u>measure</u> the sides and angles of polygons.

5. **problem** (n): a question to be solved and answered

   The last <u>problem</u> on the math quiz was the hardest.

6. **polygon** (n): a geometric figure with three or more angles and sides

   A triangle is an example of a <u>polygon</u>.

7. **equal** (adj): having the same amount, quantity, or value

   One dollar and four quarters are <u>equal</u> in value.

8. decimal (n): a number with one or more digits to the right of a decimal point

   The number 7.85 is a decimal.

9. graph (n): a drawing or diagram that shows the relationship between two or more quantities

   The graph showed how many students chose hot dogs, tacos, or pizza for lunch.

10. quotient (n): the answer to a division problem, not including the remainder

    Seth easily worked out the quotient for the division problem.

Vocabulary Tip

Understanding math words is important to learning math.

Math Words

33.1 Dinosaur Playground

Because so many fossils of dinosaurs have been found in this place, it is sometimes called "the playground of the dinosaurs." Where is this place?

To answer the question, find the word for each definition below. Choose your answers from the words after the definitions. Write the letter of each answer in the space above its definition number at the bottom of the page. You will need to divide the letters into words. One letter is provided.

1. a question to be solved and answered _____

2. having the same amount, quantity, or value _____

3. a drawing or diagram that shows the relationship between two or more quantities _____

4. a number that names a part of a whole or a part of a group _____

5. a geometric figure with three or more angles and sides _____

6. a guess or opinion about the size, amount, etc. of something _____

7. a number with one or more digits to the right of a decimal point _____

8. the answer to a division problem, not including a remainder _____

9. a unit used to find the length, width, weight, etc. of something _____

10. an answer; an explanation _____

Answers

O. quotient
N. fraction
D. solution
L. problem
T. decimal

U. equal
B. estimate
S. polygon
A. measure
K. graph

__ __ __ __ __ __ __ __ __ __ __ __ H __ __ __ __ __ __
6 9 10 1 9 4 10 5 5 8 2 7   10 9 3 8 7 9

33.2 Food and Fuel

Food provides your body with nutrients. Your body uses these nutrients to grow, to repair itself, and for energy. Four important nutrients are proteins, fats, vitamins, and minerals. A fifth nutrient is your body's main source of fuel. What nutrient is this?

To answer the question, complete each sentence below. Choose your answers from the words after the sentences. Write the letter of each answer in the space above its sentence number at the bottom of the page. One letter is provided.

1. For a figure to be a _____, it must have at least three sides and three angles.

2. You must include a point when writing a _____.

3. Ronnie helped his father _____ exactly how big the new shelves for his room could be.

4. We have to _____ about how much paint we need for the walls of the room.

5. Mrs. Jones assigned only one math _____ for homework last night.

6. A _____ tells how many parts of a whole you have.

7. The winners of the math contest in each class received prizes of _____ value.

8. No matter how hard Alana tried, she could not find the _____ to the multiplication challenge problem.

9. Danielle knows how to divide and easily finds the _____ of any division problem.

10. Eddie drew a _____ comparing the amount of rainfall for five cities.

Answers

H. equal	Y. estimate	T. measure	C. solution	D. decimal
O. polygon	A. graph	R. fraction	E. problem	B. quotient

__ __ __ __ __ __ __ __ __ __ __ __ <u>S</u>
8   10   6   9   1   7   4   2   6   10   3   5

Math Words

33.3 Montana

The name Montana comes from the Latin form of a Spanish word. What does this word mean?

To answer the question, read each sentence below. If the underlined word is used correctly, write the letter for *correct* in the space above its sentence number at the bottom of the page. If the underlined word is not used correctly, write the letter for *incorrect*. One letter is provided.

1. The <u>quotient</u> is the answer to a multiplication problem.
   A. correct   O. incorrect

2. Mario used a ruler to <u>measure</u> the sides of a rectangle.
   S. correct   N. incorrect

3. Things that are <u>equal</u> do not have the same amount.
   M. correct   N. incorrect

4. A <u>polygon</u> must have four sides.
   E. correct   A. incorrect

5. A <u>graph</u> is a way to show how two or more quantities are related.
   N. correct   E. incorrect

6. The number 25.1 is a <u>decimal</u>.
   M. correct   S. incorrect

7. When solving a math <u>problem</u>, be careful not to make careless mistakes.
   T. correct   E. incorrect

8. A <u>fraction</u> of the students of the class chose not to go on the trip.
   U. correct   I. incorrect

9. An <u>estimate</u> is always an exact number.
   L. correct   U. incorrect

10. The <u>solution</u> is the first step to finding the answer to a problem.
    A. correct   O. incorrect

—   —   —   —   —   —   I   —   —   —   —
6   1   8   3   7   4   5   10   9   2

Math Words

Geography Words

G eography is the study of the earth and its features.

1. continent (n): one of the earth's seven major land masses

   North America is a <u>continent</u>.

2. mountain (n): a natural elevation of land, usually rising to a peak

   Mount Everest is the highest <u>mountain</u> in the world.

3. river (n): a large natural stream of water that flows into an ocean or another body of water

   The flood caused the <u>river</u> to overflow its banks.

4. ocean (n): any of the four large bodies of salt water on the earth's surface

   The Pacific is the largest <u>ocean</u> on earth.

5. prairie (n): a large area of flat land with few trees and much grass; a plain

   Settlers traveled across the <u>prairie</u> in wagon trains.

6. island (n): an area of land surrounded by water

   Hawaii is an <u>island</u>.

7. plateau (n): an elevated and mostly flat area of land; tableland

   The <u>plateau</u> was a thousand feet higher than the surrounding land.

8. valley (n): low land between hills or mountains

   The town was located in the <u>valley</u>.

9. waterfall (n): a river or stream of water that falls from a high place

    Niagara Falls is a famous <u>waterfall</u>.

10. fertile (adj): rich; fruitful; productive; describing soil able to produce many crops

    The farmer's land was <u>fertile</u>.

Vocabulary Tip

Geography words help you to describe the physical features of the earth.

34.1 Fossil Fuels

Fossil fuels were formed in the earth over millions of years. We obtain much of our energy from fossil fuels. What are the fossil fuels?

To answer the question, find the word for each definition below. Choose your answers from the words after the definitions. Write the letter of each answer in the space above its definition number at the bottom of the page. You will need to divide the letters into words. One letter is provided.

1. rich; fruitful; productive; describing soil able to produce many crops _____

2. low land between hills or mountains _____

3. a natural elevation of steep land, usually rising to a peak _____

4. a river or stream of water that falls from a high place _____

5. a large area of flat land with few trees and much grass; a plain _____

6. an elevated and mostly flat area of land _____

7. one of the earth's seven major land masses _____

8. any of the four large bodies of salt water on the earth's surface _____

9. an area of land surrounded by water _____

10. a large natural stream of water that flows into an ocean or another body of water _____

Answers

C. waterfall   I. valley
O. plateau   S. mountain
R. continent   U. fertile
L. island   N. prairie
A. river   G. ocean

__ __ __ __ __ T __ __ __ __ __ __ __ __ __ __ __
6 2 9 5 10   1 7 10 9 8 10 3 4 6 10 9

34.2 A Math Helper

This device was invented in 1972. It made computing numbers easy. What was it?

To answer the question, read each sentence below. Replace the underlined word or phrase with the correct word. Choose your answers from the words after each sentence. Write the letter of each answer in the space above its sentence number at the bottom of the page. One letter is provided.

1. In the middle of the lake was a small area of land.
   R. plateau   M. river   N. island

2. The low land between the mountains was covered with small farms.
   T. valley   R. prairie   L. plateau

3. We traveled by boat down the large stream of water to the ocean.
   U. waterfall   E. river   I. island

4. The rich soil was suitable for growing many different kinds of crops.
   S. plateau   U. continent   D. fertile

5. We climbed the steep, rising land to its peak.
   R. mountain   N. plateau   S. waterfall

6. European explorers crossed the large body of salt water to reach the New World.
   E. valley   A. ocean   U. river

7. The tableland rose up from the low lands around it and stretched for miles.
   S. valley   L. plateau   R. island

8. Asia is the biggest one of the major land masses.
   O. continent   E. island   U. mountain

9. They walked through the tall grass of the plain.
   K. plateau   S. mountain   C. prairie

10. We took pictures of the stream of water falling from the high place.
    P. river   M. island   H. waterfall

___ ___ ___ ___ ___ ___ ___ ___   ___ ___ ___ ___ U ___ ___ ___ ___ ___
10   6   1   4   10   3   7   4   9   6   7   9   7   6   2   8   5

34.3 Daffy Duck

Daffy Duck first appeared in a cartoon in 1937. What was the title of this cartoon?

To answer the question, complete each sentence with the correct word. Choose your answers from the words after the sentences. Write the letter of each answer in the space above its sentence number at the bottom of the page. You will need to divide the letters into words. Some letters are provided.

1. The town was located in a _____ between mountains.

2. The _____ flowed for hundreds of miles before reaching the ocean.

3. A boat was the only way to reach the _____.

4. A _____ is a major land mass.

5. The farmer's crops grew quickly in the _____ soil.

6. The _____ was like a small mountain with its top cut off.

7. The peak of the _____ was capped with snow.

8. The wagon train rolled westward through the tall grass of the _____.

9. My grandmother lives near the coast, close to the _____.

10. The water that flowed over the cliff made a beautiful _____.

Answers

T. fertile   C. valley
Y. waterfall   D. ocean
O. island   P. plateau
K. mountain   R. river
U. continent   N. prairie

__ __ __ __ __ 'S __ __ __ __ H __ __ __
6   3   2   7 10   9   4   1   7   4   8   5

Social Studies Words

Social studies is the study of relationships between people and countries.

1. **voyage** (n): a journey over water or through the air or space

   The <u>voyage</u> from England to the American colonies took many weeks.

2. **explorer** (n): a person who searches for the purpose of discovery

   Christopher Columbus was an <u>explorer</u> who sought a sea route to Asia.

3. **citizen** (n): a member of a nation

   The rights of every <u>citizen</u> in the United States are protected by law.

4. **armada** (n): a large fleet of armed ships

   The Spanish sent an <u>armada</u> to attack England in 1588.

5. **pioneer** (n): a person who goes into an unknown land to live

   The life of a <u>pioneer</u> was hard.

6. **colony** (n): a group of people who settle in a distant land but remain under the control of their home country

   The new <u>colony</u> faced many hardships.

7. **nation** (n): a group of people who live together under the same government and share many of the same customs and usually the same language; a country

   Australia is a <u>nation</u> that is also a continent.

8. patriot (n): a person who loves and is willing to defend his or her country

   Paul Revere was an American <u>patriot</u>.

9. union (n): the joining of two or more things or people into one

   The 13 colonies formed a new <u>union</u> after the Revolutionary War.

10. frontier (n): land beyond a settled part of a country; an area that is being explored

    The <u>frontier</u> was a land of endless forests.

Vocabulary Tip

Many social studies words focus on history.

35.1 Rings Around the Planets

At one time, Saturn was the only planet thought to have rings. Its rings were made of particles of rocks, dust, and ice. Today, astronomers know that other planets in our solar system also have rings. What are three of these planets?

To answer the question, find the word for each definition below. Choose your answers from the words after the definitions. Write the letter of each answer in the space above its definition number at the bottom of the page. You will need to divide the letters into words.

1. a person who loves and is willing to defend his or her country _____

2. a person who goes into an unknown land to live _____

3. a member of a nation _____

4. a journey over water or through the air or space _____

5. land beyond a settled part of a country _____

6. a group of people who live together under the same government and share many of the same customs and usually the same language _____

7. a group of people who settle in a distant land but remain under the control of their home country _____

8. a person who searches for the purpose of discovery _____

9. the joining of two or more things or groups into one _____

10. a large fleet of armed ships _____

Answers

S. pioneer	E. frontier	R. colony	N. armada	U. voyage
T. nation	J. union	I. citizen	P. explorer	A. patriot

___ ___ ___ ___ ___ ___ ___ ___ ___ ___ ___ ___ ___
10 5   8   6   4   10 5   4   7   1   10 4   2

___ ___ ___ ___ ___ ___ ___
9   4   8   3   6   5   7

35.2 A Very Young Author

This author was only 11 years old when she wrote her first novel, *Swordbird*. Who is she?

To answer the question, complete each sentence with the correct word. Choose your answers from the words after each sentence. Write the letter of each answer in the space above its sentence number at the bottom of the page.

1. English is the most common language spoken in our _____.
   I. pioneer   A. nation   E. citizen

2. The general called upon every _____ to fight against the invaders.
   A. patriot   E. pioneer   O. explorer

3. The _____ searched for a lost city of gold.
   E. frontier   C. explorer   A. citizen

4. A human _____ to another planet is not yet possible.
   E. nation   A. frontier   I. voyage

5. The United States is a _____ of 50 states.
   N. union   S. frontier   M. colony

6. My uncle recently became a _____ of the United States.
   U. frontier   N. citizen   R. pioneer

7. William Penn founded the _____ of Pennsylvania.
   Y. colony   S. nation   H. union

8. A _____ must be courageous to build a home in an unknown land.
   R. patriot   C. voyage   N. pioneer

9. Settlers made their way to the _____ to start new lives.
   D. voyage   S. union   F. frontier

10. A large _____ sailed off to war.
    S. voyage   Y. armada   D. colony

__	__	__	__	__	__	__	__	__	__
8	1	6	3	10	7	4	9	2	5

35.3 First Inauguration

An inauguration is a president's formal introduction to office. Unlike most presidents, George Washington did not have his inauguration in Washington, DC. Where was George Washington's inauguration held?

To answer the question, read each sentence below. If the underlined word is used correctly, write the letter for *correct* in the space above its sentence number at the bottom of the page. If the underlined word is not used correctly, write the letter for *incorrect*. You will need to reverse the order of the letters and divide the letters into words. One letter is provided.

1. In terms of population, China is the largest <u>nation</u> in the world.
   I. correct   E. incorrect

2. Scientists often call space the new <u>frontier</u>.
   N. correct   P. incorrect

3. A <u>citizen</u> is not a member of any country.
   D. correct   R. incorrect

4. A <u>union</u> is a joining of only two people or things.
   I. correct   W. incorrect

5. Our <u>voyage</u> to the mall was a 10-minute drive.
   I. correct   T. incorrect

6. In the future, humans may build a <u>colony</u> on Mars.
   E. correct   H. incorrect

7. The <u>patriot</u> was willing to fight to defend his country.
   Y. correct   L. incorrect

8. The goal of an <u>explorer</u> is to find a new home.
   P. correct   C. incorrect

9. Hundreds of ships sailed in the great <u>armada</u>.
   Y. correct   I. incorrect

10. The <u>pioneer</u> traveled to the New World to find gold and then returned to the land of his birth.
    E. correct   K. incorrect

$\underline{}$ $\underline{}$ $\underline{}$ $\underline{}$ $\underline{}$ $\underline{}$ $\underline{O}$ $\underline{}$ $\underline{}$ $\underline{}$ $\underline{}$
9   5   1   8   10   3   7   4   6   2

Social Studies Words

Science Words

Science is knowledge gained from observation and experimentation and arranged in an ordered system.

1. astronomer (n): a person who studies space and the heavenly bodies

   An <u>astronomer</u> uses a telescope to study the planets.

2. predator (n): an animal that hunts other animals for food

   A lion is a <u>predator</u>.

3. element (n): A substance that has only one kind of atom

   Oxygen is a common <u>element</u> on earth.

4. atom (n): the smallest part of an element that has all the characteristics of the element

   An <u>atom</u> is far too small to see with the naked eye.

5. astronaut (n): a person who travels in space; a space explorer

   Neil Armstrong was the first <u>astronaut</u> to walk on the moon.

6. prey (n): an animal that is hunted by other animals for food

   The hawk soared over the field, looking for <u>prey</u>.

7. molecule (n): the smallest part of a substance formed by two or more atoms

   Hydrogen and oxygen combine to form a <u>molecule</u> of water.

8. atmosphere (n): the air that surrounds the earth

   The earth's <u>atmosphere</u> is made up of many gases.

9. weather (n): the state of the atmosphere at a given time

   The <u>weather</u> is sunny and pleasant.

10. climate (n): the kind of weather a place has over a long period of time

    Countries near the equator have a hot <u>climate</u>.

Vocabulary Tip

Science words help us to describe the world.

Science Words

36.1 Your Blood

Your blood carries oxygen and nutrients to the cells of your body, and it carries waste products from your cells. How much blood does the average human body contain?

   To answer the question, find the word for each definition below. Choose your answers from the words that follow the definitions. Write the letter of each answer in the space above its definition number at the bottom of the page. You will need to divide the letters into words. Some letters are provided.

1. the smallest part of a substance formed by two or more atoms _____

2. a person who studies space and the heavenly bodies _____

3. the kind of weather a place has over a long period of time _____

4. an animal that is hunted by other animals for food _____

5. the state of the atmosphere at a given time _____

6. an animal that hunts other animals for food _____

7. the smallest part of an element that has all the characteristics of the element _____

8. the air that surrounds the earth _____

9. a substance that has only one kind of atom _____

10. a person who travels in space; a space explorer _____

Answers

N. predator   U. climate
P. astronaut   G. atom
B. atmosphere   E. molecule
I. prey   T. element
H. astronomer   A. weather

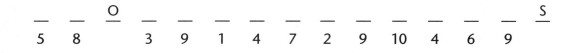

__ __ O __ __ __ __ __ __ __ __ __ __ S
5 8   3 9 1 4 7 2 9 10 4 6 9

Science Words

36.2 A Crop Scientist

One type of scientist studies soil and crops. What is the special name for this kind of scientist?

To answer the question, find the word that matches each clue below. Choose your answers from the words after each clue. Write the letter of each answer in the space above the clue's number at the bottom of the page.

1. This person flies spacecraft. What is this person?
   A. astronomer   I. predator   O. astronaut

2. It is raining outside. What is this an example of?
   R. weather   A. climate   S. molecule

3. Pure iron contains only atoms of iron. What is this an example of?
   R. prey   N. atmosphere   T. element

4. Northern Alaska has very cold winters. What is this an example of?
   A. climate   F. atmosphere   S. weather

5. This animal hunts other animals for food. What kind of animal is this?
   E. prey   T. atom   S. predator

6. This person studies the stars. What is this person?
   O. astronaut   N. astronomer   L. atmosphere

7. The smallest particle of water is made of two hydrogen atoms and one oxygen atom. What is this an example of?
   I. molecule   U. atom   E. element

8. Other animals hunt this animal for food. What is this animal?
   O. prey   I. predator   R. atmosphere

9. Gases surround the earth. What do these gases make up?
   A. astronomer   G. atmosphere   S. climate

10. This is the smallest part of an element with the characteristics of the element. What is it?
    G. prey   M. atom   O. molecule

$\overline{}$ $\overline{}$ $\overline{}$ $\overline{}$ $\overline{}$ $\overline{}$ $\overline{}$ $\overline{}$ $\overline{}$ $\overline{}$
  4   9   2   8   6   1   10   7   5   3

Science Words

36.3 A Tiny Tree

This tree grows on the tundra of Europe, Greenland, and North America. It reaches a height of only about 2 inches (5 centimeters). What is the name of this tree?

To answer the question, complete each sentence with the correct word. Choose your answers from the words after each sentence. Write the letter of each answer in the space above its sentence number at the bottom of the page. You will need to divide the letters into words. One letter is provided.

1. The hungry fox sneaked up on his _____.
   M. element   W. prey   S. predator

2. The _____ today is rainy.
   O. climate   E. atom   A. weather

3. The rocket streaked upward through the earth's _____.
   U. element   I. climate   O. atmosphere

4. A _____ must be a skillful hunter to catch other animals for food.
   I. predator   Y. molecule   A. prey

5. An _____ on Earth uses a telescope to study the planets.
   R. astronaut   F. astronomer   T. atmosphere

6. Two or more atoms can combine to form a _____.
   M. climate   C. prey   L. molecule

7. An _____ is the smallest part of an element that has all the characteristics of the element.
   D. atom   N. atmosphere   T. astronomer

8. A desert has a very dry _____.
   L. climate   N. predator   D. atmosphere

9. Gold is an _____ because the smallest part of gold is a gold atom.
   E. astronomer   W. element   R. atmosphere

10. Someday an _____ from Earth will step foot on Mars.
    W. astronaut   N. element   S. atmosphere

__	__	__	R	__	__	__	__	__	__	__
7	9	2		5	1	4	8	6	3	10

Health Words

Many words in English relate to health.

1. exercise (n): an activity that strengthens the body or mind; (v): to strengthen the body or mind

   <u>Exercise</u> is an important way to promote good health.

   Albert and his brother <u>exercise</u> at least four times each week.

2. food (n): a substance that is eaten or drunk and is necessary for the health of the body; nourishment

   Our bodies require <u>food</u> to grow.

3. jog (v): to run at a slow pace

   Mr. Carter and his wife <u>jog</u> every morning.

4. physician (n): a person trained to treat illnesses; a doctor

   The <u>physician</u> told Vanessa that she had a cold.

5. workout (n): a period of exercise

   Talia enjoyed a long <u>workout</u> in the gym.

6. fitness (n): the state of being in good physical condition

   <u>Fitness</u> is an important goal for everyone.

7. disease (n): a sickness; an illness

   The flu is a <u>disease</u> caused by a virus.

8. injury (n): a wound; damage; hurt

   Jamal suffered an <u>injury</u> during football practice.

9. heart (n): the organ in your chest that pumps blood through your body

   The doctor checked Adam's <u>heart</u> with a stethoscope.

10. checkup (n): a physical examination

    I went for a <u>checkup</u> yesterday.

Vocabulary Tip

Understanding words related to health can help you live a healthy life.

37.1 Husband and Wife Scientists

This husband and wife studied radioactivity. They contributed much to our understanding of atoms. Who were they?

To answer the question, match each word on the left with its definition on the right. Write the letter of each answer in the space above the word's number at the bottom of the page. You will need to divide the letters into words.

Words

1. fitness _____

2. jog _____

3. workout _____

4. food _____

5. exercise _____

6. injury _____

7. checkup _____

8. disease _____

9. physician _____

10. heart _____

Definitions

C. activity that strengthens the body or mind

N. a wound; damage; hurt

M. a sickness; an illness

E. the organ in your chest that pumps blood through your body

U. a period of exercise

D. state of being in good physical condition

R. a person trained to treat illnesses

I. a physical examination

A. to run at a slow pace

P. nourishment for the body

— — — — — — — — — — — — — — — — — — — —
4 7 10 9 9 10 2 6 1 8 2 9 7 10 5 3 9 7 10

37.2 Nobel Prize for a President

This president was the first American to win a Nobel Peace Prize. Who was he?

To answer the question, complete each sentence with the correct word. Choose your answers from the words after each sentence. Write the letter of each answer in the space above its sentence number at the bottom of the page. You will need to divide the letters into words. Some letters are provided.

1. To stay healthy, every year Rhonda goes for a _____.
   A. fitness   H. doctor   E. checkup

2. We _____ at least three times each week.
   N. food   T. jog   S. disease

3. Caryn's ankle _____ was not serious.
   S. checkup   Y. injury   A. heart

4. Our family's _____ helps us when we are ill.
   R. physician   M. checkup   S. food

5. When your _____ beats, it pumps blood through your body.
   F. disease   N. fitness   S. heart

6. Every living thing requires _____.
   V. food   S. injury   O. illness

7. I always feel relaxed after a _____.
   E. fitness   D. workout   A. disease

8. When you are in good physical condition, you are in a state of _____.
   T. fitness   B. exercise   J. nourishment

9. Every morning I _____ for a few minutes.
   O. fitness   L. exercise   E. checkup

10. Roberto's grandfather suffers from a serious _____.
    R. exercise   M. checkup   O. disease

```
__  __  D   __  __  __   O   __  __  E   __  E   __  __
 8   1      7   3   4    10   5      6       9   2
```

37.3 The Red Planet

Mars is often called the red planet, because it appears reddish in the night sky. What gives the Martian surface its reddish color?

To answer the question, read each sentence below. Replace each underlined word or phrase with the word that has a similar meaning. Choose your answers from the words after each sentence. Write the letter of each answer in the space above its sentence number at the bottom of the page. You will need to divide the letters into words. Some letters are provided.

1. When you run, your <u>organ that pumps blood</u> beats faster.
   I. heart   A. disease   E. illness

2. When you are ill, you should go to a <u>doctor</u>.
   O. workout   E. disease   U. physician

3. I <u>run slowly</u> three miles before breakfast every day.
   N. fitness   T. jog   S. exercise

4. The <u>injury</u> to my knee required a month to heal.
   C. exercise   S. damage   M. checkup

5. I exercise to maintain <u>a state of good physical condition</u>.
   T. workout   L. fitness   D. injury

6. We packed plenty of <u>nourishment</u> for our camping trip.
   B. injury   I. workout   S. food

7. Medicine helps doctors fight <u>disease</u>.
   K. sickness   R. checkup   D. fitness

8. A person should <u>strengthen his or her body</u> each day.
   M. fitness   H. food   R. exercise

9. Jermaine was tired after his long <u>period of exercise</u>.
   U. workout   A. fitness   E. heart

10. Everyone should have a <u>physical examination</u> once a year.
    L. wound   D. checkup   W. workout

__	__	__	T	__	__	__	E	__	__	__	__
8	9	4		5	1	7		10	2	6	3

Time Words

Many words are related to time. Without them, we would have trouble marking time.

1. calendar (n): a chart used to keep track of the days, weeks, and months

   We begin using a new <u>calendar</u> every January.

2. minute (n): 60 seconds

   Becky solved the math problem in less than a <u>minute</u>.

3. second (n): ¹⁄₆₀ minute; a brief period of time

   In the <u>second</u> that the cage was open, the canary flew out.

4. century (n): a period of 100 years

   Great progress has been made in medicine during the past <u>century</u>.

5. decade (n): a period of 10 years

   Because of my father's job, we moved three times in the past <u>decade</u>.

6. hour (n): a period of 60 minutes

   The drive to the city lasted an <u>hour</u>.

7. month (n): one of the 12 parts into which a year is divided

   Four big snowstorms hit our town last <u>month</u>.

8. year (n): a period of 365 days; 12 months

   Earth travels around the sun once in one <u>year</u>.

9. midnight (n): 12 o'clock at night; the middle of the night

   We watched the championship game on TV and did not go to bed until <u>midnight</u>.

10. noon (n): 12 o'clock in the daytime; midday

   Our lunch period starts at <u>noon</u>.

Vocabulary Tip

Many time words have been used for thousands of years.

Time Words

38.1 Utah

The name of the state of Utah comes from the Ute tribe. What was the original meaning of Utah?

To answer the question, match each word on the left with its definition on the right. Write the letter of each answer in the space above the word's number at the bottom of the page. You will need to divide the letters into words. Some letters are provided.

Words

1. month _____
2. decade _____
3. hour _____
4. calendar _____
5. second _____
6. century _____
7. midnight _____
8. minute _____
9. noon _____
10. year _____

Definitions

T. ⅟₆₀ minute

E. 12 o'clock at night

N. 12 o'clock in the daytime

U. 10 years

P. 60 seconds

L. one of 12 parts of a year

O. 365 days

S. a chart of the days, weeks, and months

A. 100 years

I. 60 minutes

___ ___ ___ ___ ___ ___ ___ F ___ H ___
 8   7   10   8   1   7   10   5   7

M ___ ___ ___ ___ ___ ___ ___
   10   2   9   5   6   3   9   4

38.2 The First American Dictionary

This man published the first American dictionary. Who was he?

To answer the question, find the word that matches each clue below. Choose your answers from the words after the clues. Write the letter of each answer in the space above its sentence number at the bottom of the page.

1. This is a length of time equal to 10 years. What is it? _____

2. Twelve of these equal a year. What is it? _____

3. One of these equals 100 years. What is it? _____

4. This is 12 o'clock at night. What is it? _____

5. This is a period of 60 minutes. What is it? _____

6. This is a chart of the days, weeks, and months. What is it? _____

7. This is a period of 12 months or 365 days. What is it? _____

8. This is 12 o'clock in the daytime. What is it? _____

9. Sixty of these equal a minute. What is it? _____

10. Sixty of these equal an hour. What is it? _____

Answers

B. second   W. minute
R. century   S. decade
H. hour   E. year
A. month   N. noon
T. calendar   O. midnight

___ ___ ___ ___   ___ ___ ___ ___ ___ ___ ___
 8   4   2   5   10   7   9   1   6   7   3

38.3 A Tasty Treat

This tasty treat was introduced in 1912. What was it?

To answer the question, complete each sentence with the correct word. Choose your answers from the words after each sentence. Write the letter of each answer in the space above its sentence number at the bottom of the page. You will need to divide the letters into words. One letter is provided.

1. The Wright brothers invented the airplane more than a _____ ago in 1903.

   A. month　　　　U. decade　　　　E. century

2. We have time to complete our science project because it is due one _____ from today.

   I. month　　　　A. second　　　　E. hour

3. I have a dentist appointment in the middle of the day at _____.

   R. noon　　　　S. midnight　　　　E. hour

4. Sarah stayed up past her bedtime and went to sleep at _____ last night.

   N. minute　　　　S. midnight　　　　R. noon

5. William practiced his trumpet for one _____ yesterday.

   T. decade　　　　C. hour　　　　M. century

6. We went on a vacation to Florida last _____.

   U. minute　　　　A. calendar　　　　O. year

7. Darren was only one _____ late, but he still missed his bus.

   E. minute　　　　T. decade　　　　O. hour

8. Jessica checked the _____ and found that the first day of spring is Saturday.

   E. month　　　　O. calendar　　　　A. year

9. James is 10 years old but tells everyone he is one _____ old.

   H. month　　　　K. decade　　　　C. century

10. A meteor streaked across the sky, but it was gone in a _____.

    S. decade　　　　M. year　　　　O. second

___　___　___　___　___　___　 O 　___　___　___　___
10　 3 　 1 　 6 　 5 　 8 　　　 9 　 2 　 7 　 4

Time Words

192

School Words, I

Some words are used often in school.

1. grade (n): a level of progress in school; (v): to evaluate or rank the quality of work

   Abby is in the fifth <u>grade</u>.

   Teachers <u>grade</u> their students' papers.

2. assignment (n): schoolwork to be completed

   Mrs. Simmons wrote our <u>assignment</u> on the board.

3. textbook (n): the standard book used in the study of a subject

   Sheryl left her science <u>textbook</u> in the library.

4. directions (n): a series of instructions

   You should always read the <u>directions</u> before starting your homework.

5. error (n): a mistake

   There was only one <u>error</u> on Mike's social studies quiz.

6. student (n): a person who goes to school

   Tamil is a <u>student</u> at Lincoln School.

7. example (n): a sample; a model

   Mr. Martinez showed us an <u>example</u> of a math problem.

8. education (n): learning, especially through school

   Education is important for success in life.

9. subject (n): something learned or taught; a topic

   Tiara's favorite subject is reading.

10. double-check (v): to look at again to find mistakes

   Our teacher encourages us to double-check our work.

Vocabulary Tip

Many of the words used in schools are also used in other areas of life.

39.1 Towering Clouds

Cumulonimbus clouds are high, towering clouds. They are usually associated with a particular kind of weather. What kind of weather is this?

To answer the question, find the word that matches each definition below. Choose your answers from the words after the definitions. Write the letter of each answer in the space above its definition number at the bottom of the page.

1. to look at again in an effort to find errors _____

2. a mistake _____

3. something learned or taught; a topic _____

4. the standard book used in the study of a subject _____

5. a sample; a model _____

6. a series of instructions _____

7. a level of progress in school _____

8. learning, especially through school _____

9. schoolwork to be completed _____

10. a person who goes to school _____

Answers

H. directions		R. error	
S. education		U. subject	
M. assignment		N. student	
E. double-check		T. example	
O. textbook		D. grade	

___ ___ ___ ___ ___ ___ ___ ___ ___ ___ ___ ___ ___
5   6   3   10   7   1   2   8   5   4   2   9   8

School Words, I

39.2 Inventor of a Hearing Aid

In 1898, Miller Reese Hutchison invented the first electric hearing aid that was worn on the body. It was the forerunner of the hearing aids of today. What was this hearing aid called?

To answer the question, complete each sentence with the correct word. Choose your answers from the words after the sentences. Write the letter of each answer in the space above its sentence number at the bottom of the page.

1. By working hard in school, you will gain an _____.

2. After reading the _____, Kevin was able to put the model together.

3. The new _____ in our class is from Texas.

4. I finished my math _____ in school.

5. My little sister is in the first _____.

6. Jared is always in a hurry and sometimes forgets to _____ his work.

7. Nick left his social studies _____ at school.

8. Studying an _____ can help you understand a problem.

9. Halley had only one _____ on her spelling test.

10. Science is Andrew's most challenging _____.

Answers

U. education   T. textbook
N. student   S. directions
O. example   I. grade
C. subject   H. error
E. assignment   A. double-check

— — —   — — — — — — — — — —
7 9 4   6 10 8 1 2 7 5 10 8 3

39.3 A Long Trip

After the sun, the next closest star to Earth is Proxima Centauri. About how many years would it take for a spaceship from Earth to travel to that star with our current technology?

To answer the question, read each sentence below. If the underlined word is used correctly, write the letter for *correct* in the space above its sentence number at the bottom of the page. If the underlined word is not used correctly, write the letter for *incorrect*. You will need to divide the letters into words. One letter is provided.

1. Raymond's math homework was on page 222 of his underlined{textbook}.
   U. correct   A. incorrect

2. Melissa corrected the only underlined{error} in her homework.
   Y. correct   E. incorrect

3. An underlined{example} should never be thought of as a sample.
   L. correct   S. incorrect

4. underlined{Education} is the study of vocabulary.
   I. correct   A. incorrect

5. Sean is the underlined{student} of the week in his school.
   T. correct   Y. incorrect

6. There are seven classes in the fifth underlined{grade} at my school.
   O. correct   I. incorrect

7. Carla did not read the underlined{directions}, so she made careless mistakes on her quiz.
   V. correct   X. incorrect

8. An underlined{assignment} is work that does not have to be completed.
   N. correct   D. incorrect

9. When you underlined{double-check} your work, you are not looking at the work again.
   T. correct   N. incorrect

10. Because we eat lunch in school, lunch is a underlined{subject}.
    R. correct   E. incorrect

$$\underline{\hphantom{x}}\ \underline{\hphantom{x}}\ \underline{\hphantom{x}}\ \underline{\hphantom{x}}\ \underline{\hphantom{x}}\ \underline{\hphantom{x}}\ \underline{\hphantom{x}}\ \underline{\hphantom{x}}\ \overset{H}{\underline{\hphantom{x}}}\ \underline{\hphantom{x}}\ \underline{\hphantom{x}}\ \underline{\hphantom{x}}\ \underline{\hphantom{x}}\ \underline{\hphantom{x}}$$

3   10   7   10   9   5   2   5   6   1   3   4   9   8

School Words, I

School Words, II

Some words are used often in school.

1. atlas (n): a book of maps and charts

   We used an <u>atlas</u> to find the states that border Iowa.

2. research (n): careful study or investigation of a topic; (v): to study or investigate a topic

   Jill finished the <u>research</u> for her report online.

   Charles will <u>research</u> Abraham Lincoln's life.

3. library (n): a room or building that contains books for reading or borrowing

   Charles borrows books from the <u>library</u>.

4. dictionary (n): a book containing an alphabetical list of words, their meanings, and their pronunciations

   Kathy looks up the meanings of new words in a <u>dictionary</u>.

5. almanac (n): a book of facts published every year

   An <u>almanac</u> is a good source of up-to-date information.

6. thesaurus (n): a book containing a list of words with their synonyms

   David checked the <u>thesaurus</u> for synonyms for *large*.

7. define (v): to state the meaning of; to explain; to describe

   We had to <u>define</u> five new words for science.

8. encyclopedia (n): a book (or set of books) containing information on a wide range of subjects

   Maria checked the <u>encyclopedia</u> for information about Jupiter.

9. compare (v): to find similarities or differences

   The reading assignment is to <u>compare</u> the traits of characters.

10. learn (v): to gain knowledge or skill

    We will <u>learn</u> about the life cycles of frogs in science today.

Vocabulary Tip

Learning vocabulary is a key to understanding any subject.

40.1 Arizona

The name Arizona comes from the Native American word *arizonac*. What is the meaning of *arizonac*?

To answer the question, find the word for each definition below. Choose your answers from the words after each definition. Write the letter of each answer in the space above its definition number at the bottom of the page. You will need to divide the letters into words.

1. to gain knowledge or skill _____
   N. library   L. learn   T. define

2. a book containing a list of words with their synonyms _____
   M. atlas   C. almanac   S. thesaurus

3. to state the meaning of; to explain; to describe _____
   I. compare   P. learn   R. define

4. a room or building that contains books for reading or borrowing _____
   E. library   U. atlas   Y. thesaurus

5. a book of facts published every year _____
   O. atlas   I. almanac   A. thesaurus

6. to find similarities or differences _____
   E. define   O. research   N. compare

7. a book (or set of books) containing information on a wide range of subjects _____
   L. encyclopedia   S. atlas   M. thesaurus

8. a book containing an alphabetical list of words, their meanings, and their pronunciations _____
   R. almanac   P. dictionary   U. atlas

9. a book of maps and charts _____
   G. atlas   C. almanac   W. thesaurus

10. careful study or investigation of a topic _____
    N. define   P. library   T. research

___ ___ ___ ___ ___ ___ ___ ___ ___ ___ ___ ___
 7   5   10 10   1   4   2   8   3   5   6   9

40.2 A Special Map

One kind of map shows the physical features of a place. What kind of map is this?

To answer the question, complete each sentence with the correct word. Choose your answers from the words after each sentence. Write the letter of each answer in the space above its sentence number at the bottom of the page. One letter is provided.

1. Hidecki's only homework was to _____ 10 words.
   A. define   E. dictionary   U. library

2. To find the location of Mexico City, Chris checked the _____.
   S. thesaurus   P. research   H. atlas

3. Anna borrowed three books from the _____.
   P. library   R. almanac   K. research

4. I would like to _____ to play the piano.
   E. define   C. learn   N. compare

5. The _____ has information on countless subjects and topics.
   T. atlas   I. dictionary   G. encyclopedia

6. When Ryan does not understand a word, he checks its meaning in a _____.
   P. dictionary   B. research   W. library

7. In science we had to _____ different plants.
   V. learn   R. compare   M. atlas

8. Deb uses a _____ to find words that have similar meanings.
   L. dictionary   R. library   T. thesaurus

9. To find the amount of rainfall in major cities last year, Jon checked an _____.
   I. almanac   O. atlas   E. encyclopedia

10. Erica began her _____ on the solar system right after school.
    U. library   O. research   I. learn

__	__	__	O	__	__	__	__	__	__	__
8	10	6		5	7	1	3	2	9	4

40.3 A Horseback Rider

There is a special word for a person who rides a horse. What is this word?

To answer the question, read each sentence below. If the underlined word is used correctly, write the letter for *correct* in the space above its sentence number at the bottom of the page. If the underlined word is not used correctly, write the letter for *incorrect*.

1. Every Saturday, Brittany goes to the <u>library</u> to borrow a new book to read.
   E. correct   U. incorrect

2. You can find the meanings and pronunciations of words in an <u>almanac</u>.
   A. correct   I. incorrect

3. A <u>thesaurus</u> is an excellent book for finding words with similar meanings.
   U. correct   E. incorrect

4. Angela spent several hours doing <u>research</u> for her report.
   N. correct   S. incorrect

5. An <u>encyclopedia</u> is a book that contains information on one topic.
   H. correct   R. incorrect

6. When you need to find the meaning of a word, you should check a <u>dictionary</u>.
   E. correct   O. incorrect

7. We <u>learn</u> new things in school every day.
   A. correct   U. incorrect

8. An <u>atlas</u> is a book of stories about other countries.
   E. correct   S. incorrect

9. To <u>define</u> a word, you must go to a library.
   W. correct   T. incorrect

10. When you <u>compare</u> two things, you can always expect them to be similar.
    N. correct   Q. incorrect

$$\overline{}\ \ \overline{}\ \ \overline{}\ \ \overline{}\ \ \overline{}\ \ \overline{}\ \ \overline{}\ \ \overline{}\ \ \overline{}\ \ \overline{}$$
   6   10   3   1   8   9   5   2   7   4

Music Words

People have played, sung, and enjoyed music for thousands of years.

1. concert (n): a musical program in which one or more singers or players perform

   We went to our school's spring <u>concert</u>.

2. audience (n): a group of people who watch or listen to something, for example, a musical performance

   A large <u>audience</u> listened to the band.

3. musician (n): a person who writes and/or performs music

   Jenna is a wonderful <u>musician</u> who sings and plays the guitar.

4. harmony (n): an enjoyable combination of musical sounds

   The <u>harmony</u> of the members of the glee club was excellent.

5. piano (n): a large musical instrument played by striking keys

   Jacob likes playing the <u>piano</u>.

6. orchestra (n): a large group of musicians who play together

   The fifth grade <u>orchestra</u> played five songs at the school play.

7. composer (n): a person who writes music

   Randy's uncle is a <u>composer</u> who has written more than one hundred songs.

8. duet (n): a musical composition written for two performers; a pair of musicians who perform together

   Kendall and his brother sang a <u>duet</u> at their school's talent show.

9. trio (n): a group of three musicians or performers

   The three friends formed a singing <u>trio</u>.

10. conductor (n): a person who directs an orchestra

    The <u>conductor</u> led the orchestra during the song.

Vocabulary Tip

When people speak or write about music, they often use *music* words.

Music Words

© Gary Robert Muschla

41.1 First for a Gymnast

This American gymnast won a gold medal in the 1984 Summer Olympics. She then became the first woman to appear on the cover of a Wheaties box. Who is she?

To answer the question, find the word that matches each definition below. Choose your answers from the words after the definitions. Write the letter of each answer in the space above its definition number at the bottom of the page.

1. a large musical instrument played by striking keys _____

2. a musical program in which one or more singers or players perform _____

3. a large group of musicians who play together _____

4. a person who writes and/or performs music _____

5. a group of three musicians or performers _____

6. a person who writes music _____

7. an enjoyable combination of musical sounds _____

8. a group of people who watch or listen to something; for example, a musical performance _____

9. a person who directs an orchestra _____

10. a musical composition written for two performers; a pair of musicians who perform together _____

Answers

T. conductor   O. trio   M. duet
Y. composer   R. harmony   A. orchestra
E. piano   U. concert   L. audience
N. musician

__ __ __ __   __ __ __   __ __ __ __ __ __
10   3   7   6   8   5   2   7   1   9   9   5   4

41.2 A Famous Nursery Rhyme

In 1806, this woman wrote the words of "Twinkle, Twinkle, Little Star." Who was she?

To answer the question, complete each sentence with the correct word. Choose your answers from the words after each sentence. Write the letter of each answer in the space above its sentence number at the bottom of the page.

1. The voices of the singers blended together in perfect _____.
   S. audience   L. harmony   U. orchestra

2. The two singers performed as a _____.
   E. trio   W. composer   A. duet

3. Tyler loves music and wants to be a _____ someday.
   I. concert   A. musician   O. melody

4. Haley's aunt taught her how to play the _____.
   R. piano   Y. orchestra   N. audience

5. The summer _____ was held in a park.
   A. composer   E. concert   K. harmony

6. The _____ directed the orchestra throughout the performance.
   O. conductor   E. audience   I. concert

7. The _____ wrote music for several singers.
   T. harmony   S. concert   J. composer

8. The _____ waited for the band to start playing.
   S. piano   T. audience   C. melody

9. The _____ was made up of over 100 musicians.
   Y. orchestra   J. duet   E. composer

10. The members of the _____ were three sisters.
    S. duet   H. orchestra   N. trio

__ __ __ __   __ __ __ __ __ __
7   2   10 5   8   3   9   1   6   4

41.3 One of the Seven Dwarfs

The seven dwarfs are famous characters in Disney's movie *Snow White*. Of the seven dwarfs, only Dopey's face can be described in this way. How can Dopey's face be described?

To answer the question, read each sentence below. If the underlined word is used correctly, write the letter for *correct* in the space above its sentence number at the bottom of the page. If the underlined word is not used correctly, write the letter for *incorrect*. You will need to divide the letters into words.

1. Alisha plays three instruments, but her favorite is the <u>piano</u>.
   N. correct   R. incorrect

2. Tickets for the <u>concert</u> were sold out.
   E. correct   A. incorrect

3. The three members of the <u>duet</u> were best friends.
   H. correct   S. incorrect

4. The <u>musician</u> did not write music, sing, or play an instrument.
   E. correct   R. incorrect

5. The <u>orchestra</u> had only one musician.
   O. correct   A. incorrect

6. The <u>audience</u> loved the singer's new song.
   H. correct   T. incorrect

7. A <u>trio</u> may have three or more members.
   N. correct   D. incorrect

8. The <u>composer</u> wrote many songs.
   O. correct   E. incorrect

9. The group sang in wonderful <u>harmony</u>.
   A. correct   U. incorrect

10. It is not the job of the <u>conductor</u> to lead an orchestra.
    M. correct   B. incorrect

___ ___ ___ ___ ___ ___ ___ ___ ___ ___
 6   9   3   1   8   10   2   5   4   7

Travel Words

Whenever you go from one place to another, you may use travel words.

1. vacation (n): a length of time for pleasure, rest, or relaxing

   We went to Disney World for our <u>vacation</u> last summer.

2. journey (n): a voyage or trip; (v): to go to a place

   A future <u>journey</u> to Mars will take about ten months.

   Someday humans will <u>journey</u> to the stars.

3. tourist (n): a person who travels for pleasure

   The <u>tourist</u> from France took photographs of New York City.

4. cruise (n): a sea voyage for enjoyment; (v): to travel or sail about

   We went on a <u>cruise</u> to Florida last year.

   The ship will <u>cruise</u> the waters off Alaska.

5. traffic (n): the number of cars and trucks on a road

   <u>Traffic</u> was very heavy because of an accident.

6. airport (n): a place where airplanes take off and land

   Our plane landed at the <u>airport</u> at 6:00 PM.

7. route (n): a road, course, or way for traveling from one place to another

   The shortest <u>route</u> home was through the valley.

8. flight (n): a scheduled trip on an airplane

    Our <u>flight</u> to Houston is scheduled to leave at 2:00 PM.

9. baggage (n): luggage; suitcases

    We packed our <u>baggage</u> for our trip.

10. highway (n): a main public road

    The <u>highway</u> was the fastest way to the city.

Vocabulary Tip

The word *travel* was first used in the 14th century.

Travel Words

42.1 Other-Worldly First

On February 6, 1971, astronaut Alan Shepard became the first human to do this. What did Shepard do on that day?

To answer the question, match each word on the left with the key words of its definition on the right. Write the letter of each answer in the space above the word's number at the bottom of the page. You will need to divide the letters into words. Some letters are provided.

Words

1. cruise _____
2. vacation _____
3. baggage _____
4. route _____
5. highway _____
6. traffic _____
7. tourist _____
8. airport _____
9. journey _____
10. flight _____

Key Words of Definitions

N. a road, course, or way

E. number of cars and trucks on a road

Y. main public road

M. place for airplanes to take off and land

T. a length of time for pleasure or rest

G. luggage; suitcases

O. scheduled trip on an airplane

A. sea voyage for enjoyment

L. person who travels for pleasure

P. voyage or trip

__ __ __ __ __ __ __ F __ __ __ H __ __ __ __ __
9   7   1   5   3 10   7   10   4   2   6   8 10 10   4

Travel Words

42.2 A Little League First

In 1989, this girl became the first US girl to play in the Little League World Series. Who was she?

   To answer the question, complete each sentence with the correct word. Choose your answers from the words after each sentence. Write the letter of each answer in the space above its sentence number at the bottom of the page. One letter is provided.

1. _____ was slow with lots of cars and trucks on the road.

   B. Flight   T. Traffic   E. Tourist

2. Every year we go to the mountains for a relaxing _____.

   K. vacation   U. baggage   S. cruise

3. The speed limit on the _____ was 60 miles per hour.

   A. highway   R. flight   I. vacation

4. Our mail person has a _____ he follows each day.

   E. flight   A. cruise   O. route

5. Planes were landing and taking off at the big _____.

   S. highway   C. airport   M. journey

6. Because of the snowstorm, our _____ did not take off on time.

   J. airport   W. traffic   B. flight

7. The _____ enjoyed visiting London.

   O. flight   E. tourist   I. traffic

8. My Uncle Bill wants to take a _____ around the world.

   I. journey   Y. highway   N. baggage

9. We looked forward to our _____ to the island.

   R. cruise   L. arrive   C. tourist

10. We had a lot of _____ because we brought so many clothes on our trip.

   S. traffic   M. cruise   V. baggage

   __ __ __ __ __ __ __ __   __ __   __ __ __ __
   10   8   5   1   4   9   8   3   6   9   5   2   7   9
                                            U

Travel Words

42.3 Houseflies

Houseflies are fast-flying bugs. Just try to swat one. How many times does a housefly beat its wings per second?

To answer the question, read each sentence below. Replace each under-lined word or phrase with the word or phrase that has a similar meaning. Write the letter of each answer in the space above its sentence number at the bottom of the page. You will need to divide the letters into words. Some letters are provided.

1. The person who travels for pleasure saw the Statue of Liberty.

   M. journey   C. flight   T. tourist

2. The four-lane main public road connected several cities.

   A. cruise   T. highway   Y. traffic

3. We spent our length of time for pleasure and rest at a lake.

   E. vacation   O. journey   U. baggage

4. Our scheduled trip on an airplane left on time.

   R. traffic   N. flight   H. cruise

5. We were late because of the high numbers of cars and trucks on the road.

   I. highway   S. journey   O. traffic

6. Rosalie put the luggage in the trunk of her car.

   D. baggage   Y. vacation   N. cruise

7. During Colonial days, a voyage from Europe to the New World took weeks.

   B. journey   R. vacation   K. flight

8. Tony's father works at a place where airplanes take off and land.

   N. a highway   U. an airport   S. a cruise

9. The course for the race went through the park.

   A. route   I. cruise   E. traffic

10. Our family is looking forward to a <u>sea voyage for enjoyment</u> this summer.

    E. flight   H. tourist   R. cruise

                                W   H

 — — — — — — — —   — — — — — —

 9   7   5   8   1   2   5   8   4   6 10 3   6

Sports Words

Sports are popular the world over. People both take part in and watch sporting events.

1. player (n): a member of a sports team; a person who plays in a game

    James is the youngest <u>player</u> on the hockey team.

2. teammate (n): someone who is on the same team as another person

    Carin is Bekka's <u>teammate</u> in soccer.

3. coach (n): a person who manages a team or trains the team's members

    Mrs. Hays is the <u>coach</u> of the girls' basketball team.

4. practice (n): training by doing the same thing again and again; (v): to do something again and again to become skilled at it

    Soccer <u>practice</u> will start right after school.

    The basketball team will <u>practice</u> shooting today.

5. score (n): the number of points (runs, goals, touchdowns, etc.) by a team or person in a game; (v): to gain a point in a game

    The Tigers won by a <u>score</u> of 3 to 2.

    Roger hoped to <u>score</u> a goal in the hockey game.

6. fan (n): a supporter of a person or team in a game

    Ruiz is a <u>fan</u> of the Yankees.

7. winner (n): a person or team with the best score in a game

    The <u>winner</u> of the tennis match won a gold medal.

8. athlete (n): a person who takes part in competitive sports

   Kristen is an <u>athlete</u> who plays lots of sports.

9. league (n): an organized group of sports teams that play against each other

   Chaz plays in a soccer <u>league</u> for third, fourth, and fifth graders.

10. equipment (n): the materials and objects players and teams use in sports

    Helmets are an important piece of <u>equipment</u> for many sports.

Vocabulary Tip

Every sport has its own special words.

43.1 A President's Middle Name

This president is best known by his middle and last names. Who was he?
   To answer the question, find the word that matches each definition below. Choose your answers from the words after the definitions. Write the letter of each answer in the space above its definition number at the bottom of the page. You will need to divide the letters into words. Some letters are provided.

1. the number of points (runs, goals, touchdowns, etc.) by a team or person in a game _____

2. training by doing the same thing again and again _____

3. an organized group of sports teams that play against each other _____

4. a supporter of a person or team in a game _____

5. the materials and objects players and teams use in sports _____

6. a person who takes part in competitive sports _____

7. a member of a sports team; a person who plays in a game _____

8. a person or team with the best score in a game _____

9. a person who manages a team or trains the team's members _____

10. someone who is on the same team as another person _____

Answers

A. equipment   S. league
D. fan   H. score
T. athlete   O. teammate
W. player   I. coach
L. winner   N. practice

__ __ __ M __ __ __ __ __ __ R __ __ __ __ __ __ __ __ __
6   1 10   5 3 7 10 10 4   10 7 7 9 8 3 10 2

43.2 A Not-so-Famous Bear

Cindy Bear is not as well-known as some bears. Who is she?

To answer the question, complete each sentence with the correct word. Choose your answers from the words after each sentence. Write the letter of each answer in the space above its sentence number at the bottom of the page. You will need to divide the letters into words. Some letters are provided.

1. The _____ of the football team got the team ready for the game.

   E. fan   A. coach   H. winner

2. The Eagles lost the game by a _____ of 8 to 7.

   D. score   N. practice   H. winner

3. A glove is an important piece of _____ for a baseball player.

   S. practice   M. score   B. equipment

4. Lindsay is an excellent _____ who plays three competitive sports.

   F. athlete   E. winner   N. fan

5. Our town's junior soccer _____ has ten teams.

   S. coach   E. league   Y. equipment

6. Marta is the best _____ on the soccer team.

   O. player   L. fan   R. winner

7. John's brother is also his _____ on the hockey team.

   C. player   R. teammate   J. league

8. Raphael was the _____ of the tennis match.

   W. equipment   U. practice   I. winner

9. Ashlee is a baseball _____ who watches as many games as she can.

   Y. fan   D. teammate   T. league

10. Football _____ began right after school.

   N. score   U. league   G. practice

__ __ __ L __ __ __ __ N __ __ __   __ __ __ __ __ __ __ __
10 8 7   4 7 8 5   2 6 4   9 6 10 8 3 5 1 7

43.3 A Special Baseball Player

In the *Peanuts* comic strip, this fictional person is Charlie Brown's favorite baseball star. Who is this person?

To answer the question, match each word on the left with the clue to its definition on the right. Write the letter of each answer is the space above the word's number at the bottom of the page. Some letters are provided.

Words	Clues to Definitions
1. player _____	E. points in a game
2. practice _____	L. plays competitive sports
3. score _____	O. manages a team
4. equipment _____	J. person or team with best score
5. athlete _____	S. plays on the same side in a game
6. fan _____	K. supports a team
7. league _____	H. a person who plays in a game
8. winner _____	N. materials and objects used by players in sports
9. coach _____	I. organization of teams that play against each other
10 teammate _____	B. doing something over and over again to become skilled

__ __ __   __ __ __ A__ __ __ T__ __ __ __
8 9 3   10 1 5   2 9   4 7 6

Around-the-Town Words

Towns have many things in common. This gives rise to a common vocabulary.

1. **grocery** (n): a store that sells food and household supplies

   Sara went to the <u>grocery</u> to shop for food.

2. **building** (n): a structure such as a house, school, store, etc.

   The new office <u>building</u> is four stories high.

3. **sidewalk** (n): a pathway for people to walk along a road

   The <u>sidewalk</u> was made of cement.

4. **restaurant** (n): a place that serves meals to customers

   Maria's parents own an Italian <u>restaurant</u>.

5. **community** (n): a group of people living in the same area, such as a town

   Our <u>community</u> always has a Memorial Day parade.

6. **business** (n): a person's work, trade, or profession to earn a living

   Tom's father owns a computer repair <u>business</u>.

7. **property** (n): a piece of land that is owned; something owned

   The little house was set on a big piece of <u>property</u>.

8. **hotel** (n): a place that provides lodging and may also provide food for guests

   When we went to New York City, we stayed in a <u>hotel</u>.

9. church (n): a place for worship

   Sara and her parents go to <u>church</u> every Sunday.

10. street (n): a roadway in a city or town

    The wide <u>street</u> was lined with tall trees.

Vocabulary Tip

When we talk about towns, we use many of the same words.

44.1 Snakes

1. a structure such as a house, school, store, etc. _____

2. a place that serves meals to customers _____

3. a place for worship _____

4. a group of people living in the same area, such as a town _____

5. a place that provides lodging and may also provide food for guests _____

6. a roadway in a city or town _____

7. a person's work, trade, or profession to earn a living _____

8. a pathway for people to walk along a road _____

9. a store that sells food and household supplies _____

10. a piece of land that is owned; something owned _____

Answers

H. hotel	N. restaurant
S. building	O. business
I. grocery	T. street
W. community	G. property
U. sidewalk	E. church

__	__	__	__	__	__	__	__	__	__	__	__	__
4	9	6	5	9	6	1	6	7	2	10	8	3

Around-the-Town Words

44.2 A First for a Space Probe

In 1971, the American space probe *Mariner 9* became the first probe from Earth to do this. What did Mariner 9 do?

To answer the question, match each word on the left with the key words of its definition on the right. Write the letter of each answer in the space above the word's number at the bottom of the page. You will need to divide the letters into words. One letter is provided.

Words	Key Words of Definitions
1. church _____	N. a food store
2. business _____	R. place that provides lodging for guests
3. sidewalk _____	I. work, trade, or profession to earn a living
4. grocery _____	O. something owned
5. hotel _____	E. place that serves meals to customers
6. community _____	T. roadway
7. property _____	L. place for worship
8. restaurant _____	P. structure such as a house, school, store, etc.
9. building _____	A. a group of people living in the same area
10. street _____	H. pathway to walk along a road

$$\underset{7}{\_\_}\ \underset{5}{\_\_}\ \underset{}{\overset{B}{\_\_}}\ \underset{2}{\_\_}\ \underset{10}{\_\_}\ \underset{6}{\_\_}\ \underset{4}{\_\_}\ \underset{7}{\_\_}\ \underset{10}{\_\_}\ \underset{3}{\_\_}\ \underset{8}{\_\_}\ \underset{5}{\_\_}\ \underset{9}{\_\_}\ \underset{1}{\_\_}\ \underset{6}{\_\_}\ \underset{4}{\_\_}\ \underset{8}{\_\_}\ \underset{10}{\_\_}$$

44.3 A Game by a Different Name

In Great Britain, tic-tac-toe is known by another name. What is tic-tac-toe called in Great Britain?

To answer the question, complete each sentence with the correct word. Choose your answers from the words after each sentence. Write the letter of each answer in the space above its sentence number at the bottom of the page. Some letters are provided.

1. Gianna and her brother have a pet-walking _____.

    H. business   T. restaurant   C. hotel

2. Every Sunday the minister welcomes people to the _____.

    A. grocery   I. sidewalk   U. church

3. The _____ offered excellent lodging and food for its guests.

    N. building   H. grocery   C. hotel

4. James helped his father shovel snow from the _____ so that people would not have to walk on the road.

    T. sidewalk   D. grocery   M. business

5. Laurie went to the _____ to buy food for the week.

    V. church   R. hotel   N. grocery

6. The _____ by the river was very valuable.

    L. street   O. property   E. church

7. We drove on the _____ that went through the center of town.

    R. business   H. restaurant   D. street

8. Our _____ has a harvest celebration in the fall.

    A. community   Y. property   U. sidewalk

9. We ate dinner at a _____ last night.

    C. grocery   S. restaurant   K. street

10. The big _____ contained many stores and shops.

    G. building   N. church   T. grocery

__ __ __ __ __ __ __   __ __ __   __ R __ __ __ E __
5 6 2 10 1 4 9   8 5 7   3   6 9 9   9

Around-the-Home Words

We use many words to describe our homes.

1. apartment (n): a room or rooms people live in, usually in part of a large building

   We rent an <u>apartment</u> in a building on Main Street.

2. furnace (n): the heating unit of a building, usually burning natural gas or oil

   When our <u>furnace</u> broke down, we did not have any heat.

3. chimney (n): a tall, hollow structure through which smoke from a furnace, fireplace, or stove leaves a building

   The smoke rose from the brick <u>chimney</u>.

4. furniture (n): chairs, tables, couches, dressers, beds, etc., used in a home

   Sonya's mother bought new <u>furniture</u> for the living room.

5. neighbor (n): a person who lives next door or close by

   Mr. Morgan is our new <u>neighbor</u>.

6. ceiling (n): the top surface of a room

   Omar used a ladder to paint the <u>ceiling</u> of the room.

7. garage (n): a building or part of a house in which to park a car

   Dad parks our car in the <u>garage</u> every night.

8. garden (n): a plot of land used for growing flowers, vegetables, or fruit; (v): to grow plants such as flowers, vegetables, or fruit on a plot of land

   Aunt Margaret has a vegetable <u>garden</u> behind her house.

9. lawn (n): a yard or area of land planted with grass

   Steve mowed the <u>lawn</u> yesterday.

10. kitchen (n): a place or room where food is prepared and cooked

    We have a sink, refrigerator, stove, and microwave in our <u>kitchen</u>.

Vocabulary Tip

Many words used to describe homes trace their roots to ancient times.

45.1 A Fairy Tale Villain

In Disney's movie *Sleeping Beauty*, this woman is the villain. Who is she?
To answer the question, find the word for each definition. Choose your answers from the words after each definition. Write the letter of each answer in the space above its definition number at the bottom of the page.

1. a person who lives next door or close by _____

   M. garden   C. neighbor   E. chimney

2. a room or rooms people live in, usually in part of a large building _____

   E. apartment   O. garden   Y. kitchen

3. a building or part of a house in which to park a car _____

   R. garden   N. garage   A. neighbor

4. the top surface of a room _____

   U. apartment   K. furniture   I. ceiling

5. the heating unit of a building, usually burning natural gas or oil _____

   W. chimney   O. kitchen   L. furnace

6. chairs, tables, couches, dressers, beds, etc., used in a home _____

   E. furniture   I. apartment   R. garden

7. a place or room where food is prepared and cooked _____

   T. garage   F. kitchen   M. chimney

8. a plot of land used for growing flowers, vegetables, or fruit _____

   M. garden   J. lawn   C. furniture

9. a tall, hollow structure through which smoke from a furnace, fireplace, or stove leaves a building _____

   B. apartment   N. ceiling   T. chimney

10. a yard or area of land planted with grass _____

   U. garden   A. lawn   S. neighbor

    ___   ___   ___   ___   ___   ___   ___   ___   ___   ___
    8   10   5   2   7   4   1   6   3   9

Around-the-Home Words

45.2 The Earth's Core

The Earth's core is made mostly of two metals. What are these metals?

To answer the question, complete each sentence with the correct word. Choose your answers from the words after each sentence. Write the letter of each answer in the space above its sentence number at the bottom of the page. You will need to divide the letters into words. One letter is provided.

1. My mom likes to cook and has a big _____.

    A. kitchen   Y. garage   O. lawn

2. Mrs. Smith lives across the street and is a wonderful _____.

    U. garage   I. garden   E. neighbor

3. Our roof leaked in the rain and water dripped through the _____.

    D. ceiling   N. garden   G. furniture

4. Our new _____ makes our house warm.

    S. chimney   L. furnace   I. kitchen

5. The grass of a healthy _____ is thick and green.

    C. lawn   N. ceiling   H. furniture

6. Smoke from the wood burning in the fireplace left the house through the _____.

    A. furnace   U. kitchen   O. chimney

7. The _____ is big enough for two cars.

    V. ceiling   R. garage   D. apartment

8. The _____ in the expensive hotel was very comfortable.

    N. furniture   C. furnace   T. garden

9. Dan's _____ was on the second floor of the building.

    E. garage   R. lawn   I. apartment

10. Suzanna's mother has a _____ of beautiful flowers.

    O. kitchen   I. garden   M. lawn

___ ___ ___ ___ ___ ___ ___ ___ ___ ___ _K_ ___ ___
 9   7   6   8   1   8   3   8   10   5   2   4

45.3 Home Sweet Home

Woody Woodpecker is a cartoon character who first appeared in 1940. Where was Woody's home?

To answer the question, read each sentence below. If the underlined word is used correctly, write the letter for *correct* in the space above its sentence number. If the underlined word is used incorrectly, write the letter for *incorrect*.

1. We live in New York, but our <u>neighbor</u> lives in California.

   R. correct   L. incorrect

2. Callie's aunt lives in an <u>apartment</u> in the city.

   U. correct   H. incorrect

3. Mr. Raymond hired Jayson to cut his <u>lawn</u> once each week.

   D. correct   E. incorrect

4. We covered the <u>ceiling</u> in our family room with a carpet.

   E. correct   U. incorrect

5. Mom always cooks dinner in the <u>kitchen</u>.

   B. correct   W. incorrect

6. Smoke from a fireplace does not leave a house through a <u>chimney</u>.

   I. correct   E. incorrect

7. Larissa watered the flowers in her <u>garden</u>.

   D. correct   M. incorrect

8. The <u>furnace</u> cooled the house during the hot summer weather.

   Y. correct   G. incorrect

9. The floor of a house is an example of <u>furniture</u>.

   T. correct   P. incorrect

10. We keep so much stuff in our <u>garage</u> that we don't have room to park our cars.

   R. correct   E. incorrect

___   ___   ___   ___   ___   ___   ___   ___   ___   ___
9   2   7   3   1   6   5   4   10   8

Around-the-Home Words

Word List

ollowing are the vocabulary words and the lessons in which they appear.

accept, L. 9	atom, L. 36	canyon, L. 30
action, L. 12	audience, L. 41	cardboard, L. 24
actor, L. 12	author, L. 32	careful, L. 18
adapt, L. 10	autobiography, L. 14	careless, L. 18
adopt, L. 10	autograph, L. 14	ceiling, L. 45
advice, L. 10	avoid, L. 3	cell, L. 7
advise, L. 10	awkward, L. 1	Celsius, L. 26
agree, L. 4	baggage, L. 42	century, L. 38
agreement, L. 19	ball, L. 5	cereal, L. 26
airport, L. 42	ballet, L. 30	certain, L. 11
alarm clock, L. 24	bandit, L. 30	champ, L. 28
alley, L. 10	barometer, L. 15	character, L. 32
ally, L. 10	bear, L. 5	cheap, L. 3
almanac, L. 40	beautiful, L. 23	checkup, L. 37
ancient, L. 22	biography, L. 14	chef, L. 29
angel, L. 10	boundary, L. 2	childish, L. 19
angle, L. 10	Braille, L. 26	chimney, L. 45
apartment, L. 45	brake, L. 8	chortle, L. 27
apology, L. 15	brash, L. 27	church, L. 44
aquarium, L. 13	brave, L. 4	citizen, L. 35
aquatic, L. 13	break, L. 8	climate, L. 36
aqueduct, L. 13	breath, L. 9	close, L. 5, 8
argue, L. 3	breathe, L. 9	closing, L. 32
armada, L. 35	brunch, L. 27	clothes, L. 8
artificial, L. 23	brush, L. 6	coach, L. 43
assignment, L. 39	building, L. 44	colonel, L. 8
astronaut, L. 36	burger, L. 28	colony, L. 35
astronomer, L. 36	business, L. 44	coma, L. 9
athlete, L. 43	calendar, L. 38	comfortable, L. 18
atlas, L. 40	camper, L. 13	comical, L. 1
atmosphere, L. 36	campus, L. 13	comma, L. 9

command, L. 11
commend, L. 11
common, L. 1
community, L. 44
compare, L. 40
composer, L. 41
concert, L. 41
condo, L. 28
conductor, L. 41
conflict, L. 2
contain, L. 13
continent, L. 34
corporation, L. 13
corps, L. 13
costume, L. 11
count, L. 5
country, L. 9
county, L. 9
cruise, L. 42
curtain, L. 11
custom, L. 11
cute, L. 1
cycle, L. 14
cyclone, L. 14
dairy, L. 9
dangerous, L. 3
dazzling, L. 21
decade, L. 38
decent, L. 11
decimal, L. 33
define, L. 40
deli, L. 28
delightful, L. 4
dense, L. 20
depot, L. 29
descent, L. 11
desert, L. 5, 9
dessert, L. 9
destroy, L. 4
detail, L. 32
diagram, L. 15
dialogue, L. 32
diameter, L. 15
diary, L. 9
dictionary, L. 40
different, L. 20

difficult, L. 23
directions, L. 39
disagree, L. 17
disease, L. 37
dishonest, L. 17
dislike, L. 17
divide, L. 1
doctor, L. 18
doesn't, L. 31
double-check, L. 39
doubt, L. 3
driveway, L. 25
drowsy, L. 20
duck, L. 6
duet, L. 41
eager, L. 21
education, L. 39
element, L. 36
encyclopedia, L. 40
energetic, L. 22
enjoyment, L. 19
enormous, L. 19
enough, L. 22
entire, L. 1
envelop, L. 11
envelope, L. 11
equal, L. 33
equipment, L. 43
error, L. 39
estimate, L. 33
example, L. 39
except, L. 9
excessive, L. 21
exercise, L. 37
exotic, L. 23
expect, L. 10
expensive, L. 20
explorer, L. 35
exquisite, L. 20
Fahrenheit, L. 26
failure, L. 3
famous, L. 20
fan, L. 43
fantastic, L. 20
farther, L. 10
ferocious, L. 2

Ferris wheel, L. 26
fertile, L. 34
fiction, L. 32
finale, L. 11
finally, L. 11
fireplace, L. 25
firm, L. 3
fitness, L. 37
flashlight, L. 24
flight, L. 42
flop, L. 27
flu, L. 28
food, L. 37
fraction, L. 33
frankfurter, L. 26
frantic, L. 22
frequent, L. 21
fridge, L. 28
frontier, L. 35
full-time, L. 25
furnace, L. 45
furniture, L. 45
further, L. 10
garage, L. 45
garden, L. 45
gather, L. 4
generous, L. 22
geography, L. 14
geometry, L. 14
gigantic, L. 1
government, L. 19
grade, L. 39
grammar, L. 15
graph, L. 33
grate, L. 8
great, L. 8
grocery, L. 44
gym, L. 28
haiku, L. 29
hardship, L. 18
harmony, L. 41
hear, L. 7
heart, L. 37
here, L. 7
he's, L. 31
highway, L. 42

hole, L. 7
homework, L. 25
hotel, L. 44
hour, L. 38
human, L. 10
humane, L. 10
humble, L. 22
humorous, L. 4
hurricane, L. 30
I'm, L. 31
immense, L. 2
impatient, L. 23
impolite, L. 16
impossible, L. 16
injury, L. 37
interesting, L. 4
inventor, L. 18
island, L. 34
it's, L. 31
jog, L. 37
journey, L. 42
joyous, L. 19
judge, L. 30
justice, L. 30
kernel, L. 8
kind, L. 6
kindness, L. 19
kitchen, L. 45
knapsack, L. 30
knight, L. 8
later, L. 9
latter, L. 9
lawn, L. 45
learn, L. 40
league, L. 43
liberty, L. 1
library, L. 40
lightening, L. 9
lightning, L. 9
limerick, L. 26
loan, L. 7
locate, L. 12
lone, L. 7
loose, L. 10
lose, L. 10
loyalty, L. 4

macaroni, L. 29
mailbox, L. 25
marvelous, L. 2
math, L. 28
matriarch, L. 15
mayor, L. 30
measure, L. 33
meat, L. 7
medal, L. 11
meet, L. 7
metal, L. 11
midnight, L. 38
minute, L. 38
misplace, L. 16
misspell, L. 16
molecule, L. 36
monarch, L. 15
month, L. 38
moped, L. 27
motel, L. 27
mountain, L. 34
musician, L. 41
mustang, L. 29
mysterious, L. 22
narrow, L. 20
nation, L. 35
nearby, L. 25
neighbor, L. 45
newspaper, L. 25
night, L. 8
nonfat, L. 17
nonfiction, L. 32
nonsense, L. 4
nonstop, L. 17
noon, L. 38
obey, L. 3
ocean, L. 34
opening, L. 32
orchestra, L. 41
ordinary, L. 23
outstanding, L. 1
pair, L. 8
passed, L. 7
past, L. 7
pasta, L. 30
pastor, L. 11

pasture, L. 11
patio, L. 29
patriot, L. 35
peaceful, L. 21
peanut butter, L. 25
pear, L. 8
peculiar, L. 22
penmanship, L. 18
photograph, L. 14
physician, L. 37
piano, L. 41
pioneer, L. 35
pitcher, L. 5
plane, L. 28
plateau, L. 34
player, L. 43
playground, L. 24
pleasant, L. 21
plot, L. 32
polite, L. 4
polygon, L. 33
popular, L. 13
population, L. 13
porter, L. 12
powerful, L. 2
practice, L. 43
prairie, L. 34
precaution, L. 16
predator, L. 36
prehistoric, L. 16
present, L. 6
prey, L. 36
primitive, L. 21
problem, L. 33
prologue, L. 15
property, L. 44
proud, L. 21
prune, L. 6
pupil, L. 5
quiet, L. 10
quit, L. 10
quite, L. 10
quotient, L. 33
rage, L. 2
rash, L. 6
react, L. 12

recent, L. 9
recycle, L. 14
remain, L. 2
remarkable, L. 18
renew, L. 17
report, L. 12
research, L. 40
resent, L. 9
restaurant, L. 44
revise, L. 2
rewrite, L. 17
right, L. 7
river, L. 34
rodeo, L. 29
role, L. 8
roll, L. 8
root, L. 6
route, L. 42
sadness, L. 19
sandwich, L. 26
saxophone, L. 26
scarce, L. 22
scene, L. 8
school, L. 5
science, L. 15
score, L. 43
seat belt, L. 24
second, L. 38
seen, L. 8
selfish, L. 19
sell, L. 7
set, L. 11
setting, L. 32
sidewalk, L. 44
sit, L. 11
slight, L. 20
smash, L. 27
smog, L. 27
soggy, L. 23
solution, L. 33
sometimes, L. 24
somewhere, L. 25
spacious, L. 3
spare, L. 23
special, L. 3
spectacular, L. 23

splendid, L. 22
splurge, L. 27
squiggle, L. 27
stake, L. 8
startle, L. 1
steak, L. 8
steal, L. 7
steel, L. 7
street, L. 44
student, L. 39
subject, L. 39
subzero, L. 17
sunny, L. 19
suspect, L. 10
swallow, L. 6
sweatshirt, L. 24
tablecloth, L. 24
teacher, L. 18
tear, L. 6
teammate, L. 43
telephone, L. 17
telephoto, L. 14
telescope, L. 17
territory, L. 12
textbook, L. 39
than, L. 9
then, L. 9
thermometer, L. 15
thesaurus, L. 40
they're, L. 31
thorough, L. 11
thoughtful, L. 18
through, L. 11
tiny, L. 2
tire, L. 6
tornado, L. 30
tourist, L. 42
towering, L. 20
traffic, L. 42
transform, L. 12
transport, L. 12
trio, L. 41
umbrella, L. 29
ump, L. 28
underground, L. 16
underline, L. 16

unhappy, L. 21
uniform, L. 12
union, L. 35
unsafe, L. 16
unsure, L. 16
up-to-date, L. 24
vacation, L. 42
vain, L. 7
valley, L. 34
vein, L. 7
vigorous, L. 23
volcano, L. 26
voyage, L. 35
waffle, L. 29
waist, L. 8
waste, L. 8
waterfall, L. 34
waterproof, L. 25
way, L. 7
wear, L. 10
weary, L. 21
weather, L. 36
weekend, L. 24
weigh, L. 7
we'll, L. 31
we're, L. 31
were, L. 10
whole, L. 7
wind, L. 5
winner, L. 43
won't, L. 31
workout, L. 37
write, L. 7
yacht, L. 29
yard, L. 5
year, L. 38
you're, L. 31
you've, L. 31

Answer Key

Lesson 1

1.1   1. T 2. E 3. W 4. A 5. S 6. R 7. I 8. K 9. G 10. H
great white shark

1.2   1. A 2. O 3. S 4. E 5. N 6. I 7. D 8. H 9. R 10. L
Rhode Island

1.3   1. O 2. E 3. Y 4. I 5. F 6. X 7. J 8. L 9. H 10. B
box jellyfish

Lesson 2

2.1   1. R 2. O 3. I 4. E 5. S 6. C 7. T 8. B 9. H 10. L
Scottish border collie

2.2   1. E 2. R 3. A 4. A 5. O 6. I 7. N 8. M 9. G 10. D
Maine and Oregon

2.3   1. A 2. C 3. K 4. M 5. N 6. I 7. L 8. D 9. W 10. B
William Buckland

Lesson 3

3.1   1. E 2. R 3. A 4. A 5. S 6. O 7. R 8. B 9. L 10. P
polar bears

3.2   1. R 2. G 3. S 4. M 5. W 6. T 7. H 8. P 9. Y 10. E
the pygmy shrew

3.3   1. T 2. R 3. N 4. Y 5. A 6. S 7. I 8. G 9. P 10. M
praying mantis

Lesson 4

4.1   1. U 2. E 3. C 4. A 5. F 6. S 7. E 8. P 9. L 10. A
Peaceful Sea

4.2   1. C 2. G 3. I 4. I 5. L 6. P 7. O 8. T 9. L 10. S
pullicologist

4.3   1. H 2. E 3. S 4. O 5. E 6. R 7. R 8. C 9. D 10. T
Dorchester

Lesson 5

5.1 1. A 2. E 3. D 4. P 5. S 6. N 7. F 8. O 9. R 10. G
golden poison dart frog

5.2 1. O 2. T 3. S 4. N 5. R 6. I 7. H 8. U 9. E 10. G
eighteen hours

5.3 1. I 2. R 3. D 4. M 5. P 6. H 7. L 8. O 9. S 10. A
sloths, opossums, armadillos

Lesson 6

6.1 1. O 2. L 3. E 4. H 5. V 6. R 7. T 8. U 9. S 10. W
twelve hours (with order of letters reversed)

6.2 1. D 2. N 3. A 4. I 5. E 6. L 7. V 8. O 9. G 10. C
Calvin Coolidge

6.3 1. Z 2. E 3. D 4. O 5. I 6. V 7. A 8. G 9. R 10. N
Giovanni da Verrazano

Lesson 7

7.1 1. N 2. Q 3. S 4. Y 5. R 6. W 7. F 8. A 9. T 10. E
twenty square feet

7.2 1. O 2. E 3. A 4. R 5. T 6. B 7. K 8. M 9. S 10. R
Bram Stoker

7.3 1. A 2. G 3. S 4. C 5. I 6. N 7. T 8. O 9. V 10. L
volcanologists

Lesson 8

8.1 1. L 2. A 3. U 4. K 5. R 6. N 7. O 8. I 9. M 10. T
Mount Kilimanjaro

8.2 1. C 2. R 3. G 4. U 5. A 6. T 7. O 8. S 9. S 10. C
saguaro cactus

8.3 1. U 2. M 3. O 4. Y 5. N 6. S 7. Q 8. H 9. J 10. A
John Quincy Adams

Lesson 9

9.1 1. Y 2. B 3. E 4. E 5. N 6. N 7. O 8. B 9. S 10. N
Benny Benson

9.2 1. O 2. D 3. A 4. A 5. C 6. A 7. V 8. G 9. M 10. S
Vasco da Gama

9.3 1. E 2. I 3. T 4. E 5. H 6. L 7. R 8. M 9. A 10. R
Amelia Earhart

Lesson 10

10.1 1. O 2. S 3. E 4. M 5. M 6. J 7. D 8. I 9. N 10. A
James Madison

10.2   1. A 2. A 3. I 4. I 5. L 6. O 7. G 8. L 9. G 10. E
Galileo Galilei

10.3   1. A 2. A 3. I 4. K 5. I 6. L 7. S 8. H 9. A 10. W
Hawaii, Alaska

Lesson 11

11.1   1. E 2. I 3. O 4. Y 5. H 6. K 7. N 8. C 9. R 10. M
Chimney Rock

11.2   1. A 2. A 3. A 4. R 5. R 6. G 7. T 8. N 9. K 10. O
kangaroo rat

11.3   1. A 2. O 3. R 4. G 5. D 6. R 7. E 8. D 9. B 10. T
Robert Goddard

Lesson 12

12.1   1. L 2. U 3. O 4. S 5. M 6. D 7. E 8. N 9. R 10. A
Roald Amundsen

12.2   1. H 2. I 3. U 4. O 5. N 6. T 7. L 8. A 9. S 10. C
South Carolina

12.3   1. T 2. T 3. N 4. I 5. E 6. O 7. T 8. M 9. E 10. N
mintonette

Lesson 13

13.1   1. S 2. I 3. O 4. A 5. B 6. E 7. Y 8. C 9. D 10. L
celestial body

13.2   1. U 2. I 3. T 4. M 5. S 6. R 7. O 8. A 9. B 10. D
Bartholomeu Dias

13.3   1. N 2. T 3. E 4. T 5. I 6. H 7. N 8. E 9. N 10. E
nineteenth (with order of letters reversed)

Lesson 14

14.1   1. N 2. A 3. E 4. C 5. T 6. R 7. K 8. S 9. F 10. Y
Francis Scott Key

14.2   1. A 2. U 3. H 4. E 5. I 6. T 7. S 8. G 9. L 10. C
sight, hearing, taste, smell, touch

14.3   1. E 2. R 3. S 4. O 5. I 6. L 7. C 8. S 9. P 10. A
solar eclipse

Lesson 15

15.1   1. S 2. S 3. E 4. U 5. O 6. U 7. A 8. T 9. R 10. G
stegosaurus

15.2   1. U 2. I 3. O 4. H 5. E 6. N 7. P 8. A 9. L 10. R
an ailurophile

15.3   1. I 2. I 3. L 4. A 5. E 6. L 7. R 8. C 9. S 10. P
capillaries

Lesson 16

16.1 1. E 2. H 3. I 4. O 5. A 6. N 7. R 8. W 9. D 10. C
Richard Owen

16.2 1. U 2. H 3. A 4. R 5. E 6. T 7. D 8. S 9. O 10. N
one hundred thousand

16.3 1. A 2. U 3. S 4. G 5. E 6. N 7. S 8. S 9. S 10. L
sunglasses

Lesson 17

17.1 1. O 2. I 3. N 4. E 5. A 6. S 7. H 8. T 9. F 10. R
the rain forest

17.2 1. I 2. C 3. E 4. B 5. H 6. U 7. F 8. L 9. S 10. N
bullfinches

17.3 1. I 2. N 3. A 4. E 5. L 6. T 7. Y 8. D 9. W 10. S
Walt Disney

Lesson 18

18.1 1. C 2. O 3. V 4. S 5. R 6. N 7. I 8. A 9. G 10. E
George Washington Carver

18.2 1. A 2. E 3. H 4. L 5. N 6. S 7. U 8. O 9. J 10. P
John Paul Jones

18.3 1. I 2. M 3. H 4. M 5. N 6. S 7. O 8. U 9. T 10. R
ornithomimus

Lesson 19

19.1 1. A 2. A 3. E 4. A 5. K 6. I 7. H 8. W 9. I 10. L
Ka Lae, Hawaii

19.2 1. E 2. H 3. O 4. N 5. R 6. T 7. P 8. I 9. C 10. L
Christopher Paolini

19.3 1. E 2. I 3. I 4. L 5. L 6. A 7. H 8. D 9. P 10. H
Philadelphia

Lesson 20

20.1 1. I 2. D 3. N 4. B 5. C 6. O 7. T 8. A 9. R 10. E
border the Atlantic Ocean

20.2 1. I 2. C 3. A 4. L 5. R 6. L 7. P 8. Y 9. R 10. B
public library

20.3 1. E 2. I 3. O 4. E 5. E 6. L 7. R 8. M 9. C 10. T
ceilometer

Lesson 21

21.1 1. R 2. M 3. W 4. O 5. A 6. I 7. G 8. L 9. R 10. S
Roger Williams

21.2 1. R 2. K 3. I 4. A 5. E 6. L 7. J 8. N 9. B 10. F
Benjamin Franklin

21.3 1. O 2. O 3. O 4. S 5. R 6. D 7. A 8. N 9. S 10. I
sauroposeidon

Lesson 22

22.1 1. P 2. L 3. R 4. S 5. E 6. T 7. G 8. H 9. I 10. O
herpetologist

22.2 1. I 2. D 3. R 4. E 5. H 6. L 7. L 8. D 9. A 10. N
Daniel Handler

22.3 1. I 2. A 3. E 4. N 5. A 6. V 7. I 8. O 9. T 10. S
aestivation

Lesson 23

23.1 1. U 2. M 3. I 4. Y 5. R 6. T 7. C 8. P 9. E 10. J
Mercury, Jupiter

23.2 1. D 2. I 3. O 4. U 5. L 6. A 7. L 8. Q 9. S 10. G
liquid, gas, solid

23.3 1. A 2. P 3. I 4. O 5. C 6. T 7. R 8. N 9. P 10. T
precipitation

Lesson 24

24.1 1. P 2. H 3. A 4. I 5. O 6. L 7. G 8. T 9. S 10. E
the Age of Reptiles

24.2 1. S 2. O 3. M 4. F 5. D 6. B 7. L 8. C 9. T 10. I
District of Columbia

24.3 1. R 2. U 3. I 4. M 5. O 6. S 7. Y 8. T 9. H 10. P
hippopotamus ivory

Lesson 25

25.1 1. D 2. I 3. A 4. H 5. T 6. P 7. R 8. N 9. E 10. S
the Stars and Stripes

25.2 1. T 2. M 3. N 4. W 5. F 6. D 7. R 8. L 9. O 10. A
land of tomorrow

25.3 1. Y 2. N 3. O 4. E 5. I 6. T 7. G 8. R 9. B 10. L
ringing of the Liberty Bell

Lesson 26

26.1 1. N 2. E 3. S 4. A 5. V 6. Y 7. U 8. H 9. M 10. R
Earth, Mercury, Mars, Venus

26.2 1. D 2. C 3. A 4. P 5. J 6. H 7. N 8. B 9. R 10. E
Jean Pierre Blanchard

26.3 1. E 2. T 3. A 4. R 5. O 6. L 7. H 8. G 9. E 10. M
geothermal

Lesson 27

27.1 1. E 2. T 3. T 4. T 5. T 6. W 7. N 8. L 9. W 10. V
twelve to twenty

27.2 1. A 2. S 3. R 4. P 5. C 6. H 7. O 8. J 9. E 10. N
Josephine Cochran

27.3 1. N 2. D 3. R 4. I 5. U 6. E 7. A 8. W 9. G 10. L
Laura Ingalls Wilder

Lesson 28

28.1 1. E 2. G 3. A 4. L 5. M 6. T 7. R 8. O 9. B 10. I
marine biologist

28.2 1. N 2. A 3. T 4. R 5. I 6. E 7. M 8. E 9. H 10. R
Henrietta Maria

28.3 1. E 2. S 3. E 4. E 5. I 6. R 7. P 8. H 9. H 10. M
hemispheres

Lesson 29

29.1 1. A 2. E 3. N 4. D 5. L 6. E 7. D 8. K 9. Y 10. O
Yankee Doodle

29.2 1. E 2. G 3. I 4. G 5. N 6. A 7. U 8. S 9. G 10. L
sign language

29.3 1. D 2. S 3. N 4. H 5. E 6. G 7. R 8. T 9. P 10. O
Peter Hodgson

Lesson 30

30.1 1. C 2. M 3. S 4. O 5. L 6. I 7. N 8. T 9. A 10. F
automatic traffic signal

30.2 1. M 2. N 3. T 4. R 5. S 6. L 7. A 8. O 9. G 10. D
Old Stormalong

30.3 1. A 2. R 3. N 4. O 5. D 6. W 7. B 8. A 9. A 10. L
Baron De La Warr

Lesson 31

31.1 1. R 2. N 3. E 4. A 5. T 6. G 7. S 8. W 9. I 10. V
West Virginia

31.2 1. R 2. V 3. E 4. T 5. P 6. I 7. L 8. G 9. M 10. B
improved lightbulb

31.3 1. S 2. R 3. E 4. A 5. Y 6. P 7. H 8. O 9. B 10. T
the Boston Tea Party

Lesson 32

32.1 1. C 2. R 3. A 4. E 5. T 6. T 7. C 8. L 9. Y 10. S
static electricity

32.2 1. T 2. A 3. L 4. N 5. I 6. R 7. O 8. V 9. E 10. G
violet, green, orange

32.3 1. E 2. C 3. N 4. S 5. R 6. W 7. J 8. A 9. K 10. D
Andrew Jackson

Lesson 33

33.1 1. L 2. U 3. K 4. N 5. S 6. B 7. T 8. O 9. A 10. D
Badlands, South Dakota

33.2 1. O 2. D 3. T 4. Y 5. E 6. R 7. H 8. C 9. B 10. A
carbohydrates

33.3 1. O 2. S 3. N 4. A 5. N 6. M 7. T 8. U 9. U 10. O
mountainous

Lesson 34

34.1 1. U 2. I 3. S 4. C 5. N 6. O 7. R 8. G 9. L 10. A
oil, natural gas, coal

34.2 1. N 2. T 3. E 4. D 5. R 6. A 7. L 8. O 9. C 10. H
handheld calculator

34.3 1. C 2. R 3. O 4. U 5. T 6. P 7. K 8. N 9. D 10. Y
Porky's Duck Hunt

Lesson 35

35.1 1. A 2. S 3. I 4. U 5. E 6. T 7. R 8. P 9. J 10. N
Neptune, Uranus, Jupiter

35.2 1. A 2. A 3. C 4. I 5. N 6. N 7. Y 8. N 9. F 10. Y
Nancy Yi Fan

35.3 1. I 2. N 3. R 4. W 5. T 6. E 7. Y 8. C 9. Y 10. K
New York City (with order of letters reversed)

Lesson 36

36.1 1. E 2. H 3. U 4. I 5. A 6. N 7. G 8. B 9. T 10. P
about eight pints

36.2 1. O 2. R 3. T 4. A 5. S 6. N 7. I 8. O 9. G 10. M
agronomist

36.3 1. W 2. A 3. O 4. I 5. F 6. L 7. D 8. L 9. W 10. W
dwarf willow

Lesson 37

37.1 1. D 2. A 3. U 4. P 5. C 6. N 7. I 8. M 9. R 10. E
Pierre and Marie Curie

37.2 1. E 2. T 3. Y 4. R 5. S 6. V 7. D 8. T 9. L 10. O
Teddy Roosevelt

37.3 1. I 2. U 3. T 4. S 5. L 6. S 7. K 8. R 9. U 10. D
rustlike dust

Lesson 38

38.1 1. L 2. U 3. I 4. S 5. T 6. A 7. E 8. P 9. N 10. O
people of the mountains

38.2 1. S 2. A 3. R 4. O 5. H 6. T 7. E 8. N 9. B 10. W
Noah Webster

38.3 1. E 2. I 3. R 4. S 5. C 6. O 7. E 8. O 9. K 10. O
Oreo cookies

Lesson 39

39.1 1. E 2. R 3. U 4. O 5. T 6. H 7. D 8. S 9. M 10. N
thunderstorms

39.2 1. U 2. S 3. N 4. E 5. I 6. A 7. T 8. O 9. H 10. C
the Acousticon

39.3 1. U 2. Y 3. S 4. A 5. T 6. O 7. V 8. D 9. N 10. E
seventy thousand

Lesson 40

40.1 1. L 2. S 3. R 4. E 5. I 6. N 7. L 8. P 9. G 10. T
little spring

40.2 1. A 2. H 3. P 4. C 5. G 6. P 7. R 8. T 9. I 10. O
topographic

40.3 1. E 2. I 3. U 4. N 5. R 6. E 7. A 8. S 9. T 10. Q
equestrian

Lesson 41

41.1 1. E 2. U 3. A 4. N 5. O 6. Y 7. R 8. L 9. T 10. M
Mary Lou Retton

41.2 1. L 2. A 3. A 4. R 5. E 6. O 7. J 8. T 9. Y 10. N
Jane Taylor

41.3 1. N 2. E 3. S 4. R 5. A 6. H 7. D 8. O 9. A 10. B
has no beard

Lesson 42

42.1 1. A 2. T 3. G 4. N 5. Y 6. E 7. L 8. M 9. P 10. O
play golf on the moon

42.2 1. T 2. K 3. A 4. O 5. C 6. B 7. E 8. I 9. R 10. V
Victoria Brucker

42.3 1. T 2. T 3. E 4. N 5. O 6. D 7. B 8. U 9. A 10. R
about two hundred

Lesson 43

43.1 1. H 2. N 3. S 4. D 5. A 6. T 7. W 8. L 9. I 10. O
Thomas Woodrow Wilson

43.2 1. A 2. D 3. B 4. F 5. E 6. O 7. R 8. I 9. Y 10. G
girlfriend of Yogi Bear

43.3 1. H 2. B 3. E 4. N 5. L 6. K 7. I 8. J 9. O 10. S
Joe Shlabotnik

Lesson 44

44.1 1. S 2. N 3. E 4. W 5. H 6. T 7. O 8. U 9. I 10. G
with its tongue

44.2 1. L 2. I 3. H 4. N 5. R 6. A 7. O 8. E 9. P 10. T
orbit another planet

44.3 1. H 2. U 3. C 4. T 5. N 6. O 7. D 8. A 9. S 10. G
noughts and crosses

Lesson 45

45.1 1. C 2. E 3. N 4. I 5. L 6. E 7. F 8. M 9. T 10. A
Maleficent

45.2 1. A 2. E 3. D 4. L 5. C 6. O 7. R 8. N 9. I 10. I
iron and nickel

45.3 1. L 2. U 3. D 4. U 5. B 6. E 7. D 8. G 9. P 10. R
Puddleburg